How to Get the Hot Jobs in Business and Finance

How to Get
THE HOT JOBS
IN BUSINESS
& FINANCE

Mary E. Calhoun

PERENNIAL LIBRARY
Harper & Row, Publishers
New York, Cambridge, Philadelphia, San Francisco
London, Mexico City, São Paulo, Singapore, Sydney

This is a revised edition of a book originally published in 1985 by Overture Publishing under the title *Wall Street Warmup: How to Get Today's Most Sought-After Jobs in Business and Finance*. It is here reprinted by arrangement with the author.

First PERENNIAL LIBRARY edition published 1986.

Library of Congress Cataloging-in-Publication Data

Calhoun, Mary E.
  How to get the hot jobs in business and finance.

  Rev. ed. of: Wall Street warmup. © 1985.
  1. Job hunting—United States. 2. Business—Vocational guidance—United States. 3. Finance—Vocational guidance—United States. I. Calhoun, Mary E. Wall Street warmup. II. Title.
HF5382.75.U6C33   1986   332'.023'73   85-45625
ISBN 0-06-097033-2 (pbk.)

---

86 87 88 89 90 MPC 10 9 8 7 6 5 4 3 2 1

for the students whose eagerness to learn
and gratitude for guidance have made
this work a labor of love.

Contents

List of Figures

Acknowledgments

I am extremely grateful to those who reviewed and offered suggestions for this book: Nancy Tobin and Joe Joyce of Wellesley College, Wendy Lane of Donaldson, Lufkin, & Jenrette, Ron Clausen of the Bank of Boston, Laura Rasmussen, Susan Drane, Sam Hartwell, Bill Catlin, and many others. My student reviewers Carrie Trautwein, Elizabeth Mullen, Elizabeth Schneirov, Deborah Wahl, Nina Holst, Nami Park, and Marsha Sterling were most helpful. I thank also Debbie Kim and her fellow students for their assistance with market research. Special thanks to Stephanie Shellman, Dick Greene, Ruth Frantz and Tina Sutton for their permission to use certain material. I am fortunate to have benefited from Dot Thorne's enthusiasm for and assistance with this project. The generous assistance of Wang Laboratories, Inc. with the project, particularly the help of Kathy Hadney and Peggy McCabe, has been invaluable. And finally, I thank the outstanding staff of the Wellesley College Center for Women's Careers, who have shared their resources and expertise as generously with me as they do with their students.

Part I

Destination:
Wall Street, U.S.A.

Chapter 1

Setting Your Sights on Success

I have been poor and I have been rich.
Rich is better.
—Sophie Tucker

YOUR DESTINATION IS Wall Street, U.S.A. On Wall Street, U.S.A. are headquartered the financial services companies offering the most-coveted jobs for the brightest and best of this year's class of job seekers. Both domestic and international firms are here. Most of them are in New York City, yet hundreds are spread from coast to coast, in Boston, Washington, D.C., Atlanta, Houston, Chicago, Minneapolis, Philadelphia, San Francisco, Los Angeles, and elsewhere. Investment banks, commercial banks, stock brokerage and financial services companies, mutual funds, investment counselors, financial publications, insurance companies, securities research firms, and venture capital investors are part of this financial universe.

You are heading for Wall Street at a time when the financial services industry is booming. A few financial firms become casualties of each stock market downdraft. Competitive strains weaken others, yet overall the expansion in the number of firms, in their size, and in the career possibilities they offer, continues at great speed.

Some of you want the six-figure salaries Wall Street can offer. Others want the power and prestige that accompany the management of the financial matters of the biggest and best corporate clients. For some, the goal is the opportunity to make an impact on the economic affairs of corporate America. Some of you aren't yet really sure what you want, but know that you would rather be at the top while you find out than in the middle.

3

In this book, we assume that you want a career, not just a job. Some of the careers we will discuss require sixty-to-eighty-hour workweeks, while others are less demanding; all require incredible commitment. We assume that you're willing to make that commitment and start today to undertake a strenuous and intense program of action to assure yourself a career in a Wall Street firm.

We will talk a lot about money because, in business, money is what we use to keep score. Money is neither good nor bad; it's simply the score. Regardless of what your personal goals may have been in the past, we assume that they now include a high score in business. Your chances of achieving that score—that goal of making money—are greater on Wall Street than any-where else. A recent review of the fifty highest-paid executives included fourteen—28%—in financial firms. The average annual cash compensation for these executives was $1,575,000—more than $200,000 higher than the average for all fifty executives!

We will also assume that very few of you are or ever will be elected to Phi Beta Kappa; that very few will graduate *summa cum laude*. There is good news: those who won't are just as likely to be successful as those who will. You may not have a 3.5 GPA or attend an Ivy League school, but it doesn't make a bit of differ-ence for your success in business, nor does it block your entrance to Wall Street.

Our last assumption is even more important: that in addition to reading this book and planning to commit your time and your money to your career search, you are willing to confront your fear.

Why talk about fear when you're not afraid? It's true that you may not be afraid now, but it's only a matter of time until you will be. Many of you will even reach the point where your career search is halted because of your fear. Of course, the official rea-son won't be fear. It will be your schoolwork, your family, your part-time job, your wedding, or the hockey team.

What you must do is start now to recognize these reasons as excuses that stand between you and a high-powered business career. It's vital that you understand the fear that's behind the excuses—fear of heading out into the make-or-break world; fear of rejection; fear of not getting the job you want; fear of trying and losing.

Think about that last statement—fear of trying and losing. Do you have a fear of losing? Were you afraid that you would lose the 100-meter freestyle in the summer Olympics? Of course not, because you didn't try. The best way to avoid losing is not to compete. The best way to avoid the fear of losing is not to compete. When I was in high school, I "never" studied for exams. That way, in case I did not do well, I had an excuse—I hadn't studied! I had given myself an excuse for losing. Whether for exams, athletic competitions, or interviews, failure to prepare gives us a perfect excuse for losing—we didn't really compete.

Psychologists tell us that concentrating on the fear of losing is one way to program ourselves into failure. We tend to do whatever is uppermost in our minds: if that is losing, we are likely to lose. Apply that tendency to the game of giving yourself an excuse for losing by not trying hard enough to win, and you have a perfect recipe for failure.

Winners, on the other hand, keep the goal in mind at all times. The more tangible the goal, the better. What is your goal? A Jaguar? A Rolex watch? To be independent? To fly first class when you travel? To be on a first-name basis with the heads of General Motors and Apple Computer? Determine your goal and keep it uppermost in your mind at all times.

Now begin to visualize yourself attaining that goal: see yourself a year from now walking down the streets of the financial district, heading for another challenging day. See yourself landing the big piece of business others have long coveted. See yourself working with the top management of a *Fortune* "500" company, putting together the final details of a major deal. Lock that vision of your successful, winning self in your mind. Negative thoughts? No room—your head is too full of a winner's thoughts—your goal and the picture of yourself attaining that goal.

And the fear? Expect it, watch for it, recognize it. When it arrives, acknowledge it and then ignore it because you—a confident winner—are so eager to reach your goal that you have no intention of losing valuable time by tolerating any excuse for not taking action.

This book is a blueprint for action—your action plan to launch your career on Wall Street.

Chapter 2

Your Action Plan for Getting
The Job You Want

*Never before have we had so little time
in which to do so much.*
—*Franklin Delano Roosevelt*

Launch a Superstar Effort

EACH SPRING, as the job offers to graduating classes start to roll in, something predictable happens: the "superstars" are agonizing over whether to choose Morgan Stanley or Prudential-Bache or Mellon Bank, while all of the others are wondering how they're ever going to get an interview, much less an offer, from one of those prestigious firms. And the non-superstars say, "well, of course they got those offers—they're superstars!" They think they're getting the offers because they have good grades, they've been active in sports, or they're involved in campus activities— but the message of this chapter is that that's not why they're getting the offers:

Superstars don't get offers because they're superstars—
it's what made them superstars that makes them get offers!

You may look enviously at friends heading for first and second and third interviews, but where were you while they were working hard at getting them? Were you playing *Trivial Pursuit* while they were sending out 100 letters to potential employers?

7

Were you drinking beer while they were studying Annual Reports from those companies? Were you reading *Sports Illustrated* while they were building a network of alumni contacts in Wall Street firms?

Landing one of the super jobs requires superstar effort. The good news is that you can start to become a superstar today. Forget your grades—they're in the past. The "A" students may think that their grades alone will get them the jobs, won't apply the kind of effort you will, and will be less successful in their job hunt.

This is not an easy exercise; it is a strenuous campaign. If you cannot make the effort required to succeed in your search for one of these jobs, then you cannot do the work they require. You don't need connections or credentials; you need commitment and drive. If you're currently a student, consider job-hunting to be an additional course, one to which you will devote as much time and effort as to Quantum Physics or Econometrics. If you're not in school and not working, regard your job search as an eight-hour job.

> *Chance never helps those*
> *who do not help themselves.*
> *—Sophocles*

Buckle down and commit today to make the kind of effort that only 1% of this year's job seekers will make. Set your sights on the choicest jobs on Wall Street, and activate your plan to make sure that you're one of the select few chosen for those jobs.

Resolve that your search begins today. Regardless of the time of year, regardless of whether you're a senior or junior, thirty-three or twenty, employed or unemployed . . . today.

If you're a college senior, information gathering can begin as early as October. November is not too early to begin to mail out your letters and resumes. In December and January, your trial interviews can be under way. By February, you should actively be interviewing.

Don't wait for on-campus recruiting—there will be only a handful of jobs for hundreds or even thousands of you and your fellow students. Worse, if you don't get an offer through recruiting, it's too late! By the time recruiting starts, you should have several interviews under your belt. For your interviews with firms that only see applicants on campus, make sure you go in as a confident, seasoned interviewing veteran, not a nervous neophyte. The student who emerges from the Smith Barney interview just before yours may be Phi Beta Kappa, but it may also be her first interview, and her self-conscious chatter may set up your cool composure very nicely!

The Job Hunting Action Plan

Find Out What You Want to Do

GO TO YOUR College Placement Office/Career Center. They have books to help you decide what you want to do as well as books about fields in which you already know you have an interest. Make sure you understand such differences as those between investment banking and commercial banking; securities research analysts and analysts in investment banking; stockbrokers and portfolio managers.

If you are not a student, it's possible that a college or university near you may allow you to use their Placement Office/Career Center library, particularly if you are an alumnus. Call to ask whether this is permitted.

Build Your Own Network

Get a list of alumni in your fields of interest from your Placement Office/Career Center. Write to them and call them or try to meet with them. Your purpose is to augment the information you've gleaned from books and articles and discussions with career counselors and faculty. You can also find out if they are aware of positions in their firms or can recommend anyone else who may be able to help you. This is called *network building*, and it's vital to your job search.

When calling on these individuals, try to send a cover letter and resume in advance. Explain clearly what your purpose is in contacting them, and state that you will call them within a certain time, such as one or two weeks. Don't expect them to call you back. "I will call you in a week to discuss these questions" is an ideal ending to your letter.

Figure 1 is a sample cover letter asking for an information interview.

Information Interviews

These information interviews can often be just as effective over the telephone as in person. Particularly if you are calling individuals with whom you share some affiliation (alumnae of your college, friends of your parents, or someone to whom a faculty member has referred you), almost everyone will be willing to answer a few questions over the telephone. Figure 2 lists sample questions you can ask in your information interviews.

Under no circumstances should you drop in on someone for an information interview without an appointment. Most businesspeople will regard this as an imposition, and it may jeopardize your chances at the firm. Telephone in advance to arrange your meeting. When you call to arrange an information interview, have your questions written down in advance. Be organized and considerate of the other person's time. Refer to your letter: "Mr. Jones, my name is John Smith. I'm calling with regard to my letter of January 10th." Ask if they have time to answer a few questions or if they can refer you to someone who can. Don't just say, "I'm calling because Alfred Jones said I should talk to you," or "I'm calling because I'm interested in banking," period.

Although I try to be helpful to those who call me for advice, the people who turn me off instantly are those who give me no questions or reasons for calling beyond "I'm interested in finance." Will I pick up the ball and carry it for them? Probably not. But for the well-organized person who says, "I'm interested in investment banking and wonder if you have time to answer several questions," I become an eager participant in the project. As well-thought-out and intelligent questions are asked ("what investment banking opportunities are there outside of New York City? What happens if I decide not to go to business school after two years as a Financial Analyst?"), I'll probably become so interested in her career search that I'll offer additional ideas that I think may be helpful, will share any job leads that have come my way, and may well invite her to lunch to discuss her career at length.

Figure 1

Sample Cover Letter for an Information Interview

Jackson Hall
Northern University
Pittsburgh, PA 15222
November 10, 1984

Ms. Anne L. Wilson
Vice President
Massachusetts Bank and Trust Company
One Financial Square
Boston, MA 02110

Dear Ms. Wilson,

I am a senior at Northern University. George Johnson of our Placement Office has told me that you have been most helpful to students seeking careers in international banking.

I am majoring in Economics with a minor in Spanish. Working for Bay-Banks during my last summer vacation has strengthened my interest in a career in commercial banking.

As you will see from my resume, which is enclosed, my primary extra-curricular interests are being Co-Captain of the Northern tennis team and participating as an active member of the Drama Club.

I hope that we may arrange a time when I may ask your advice concerning how I can best apply my Economics major and language fluency to a career in international commercial banking.

I shall contact you shortly to arrange an appointment.

Sincerely yours,

John M. Smith

Figure 2

Questions to Ask in an Information Interview

1. How would you describe your job?

2. How much client contact do you have?

3. How much traveling do you do? How do you feel about that?

4. How much contact do you have with others inside your firm?

5. What do you like most about your job?

6. What do you like least about your job?

7. How many hours a week do you work? Do you work on weekends?

8. What do you see yourself doing in five years? Ten years?

9. Can you give me a rough idea of salary levels in your industry or firm after five years? Ten years?

10. Do you think your firm or type of firm is a good training ground?

11. How much freedom do you have in terms of deciding what you want to work on and how to plan the project?

12. Do you have sufficient flexibility in your job so that you think it is possible to balance parenthood with your career?

13. Does your firm have entry-level positions available now?

14. What important changes are occurring in your field?

15. How will these changes affect your career?

16. How will they affect the career of someone like mysel just starting out in the field?

17. What type of person is most successful in your field?

18. What suggestions can you give me for obtaining an entry-level position in your field?

These information interviews, whether by phone or in person, are important to you. They are the foundation of your current and future network of contacts in business. They will also sharpen your interviewing skills and help give you that highly-desired aura of quiet confidence.

One further note on calling to arrange an information interview: don't call it an information interview. Some people are burned out by the job seekers who have called on them and taken up large amounts of time. Somehow, "information interview" connotes "I'm going to do all of the taking and you're going to do all of the giving." Avoid setting up an avoidance reaction in the person with whom you're seeking the interview, and just say, "I have a few questions." It may well end up taking just as much time as an "information interview," but it sounds much shorter!

Ask for Referrals

In despair because your next-door neighbor is the son of the Chairman of the Board of a major New York City commercial bank, and you don't seem to have any connections at all? Relax—it makes no difference as long as you're willing to make the effort to build your own network by following the steps we've outlined. In fact, your neighbor will probably rely too heavily on his connections and fail to implement an action plan such as yours that will really produce results!

> *Leave no stone unturned.*
> *—Euripides*

Asking for referrals is one of the key elements in network building. Each time you speak with someone, ask the person to give you the name of someone else who might help you. After a conversation with an alumna during which you've gathered information about your intended field, end the conversation by asking, "can you suggest anyone else with whom I should talk, or anyone who might know of some openings?" Particularly if the person has been unable to help you, this is extremely important. Almost everyone, no matter how pressed for time, wants to help you in some way. Giving you someone else's name is the easiest possible way for them to help you. Whenever someone says, "I can't help you," a buzzer should go off in your head, activating an instantaneous response: "Do you perhaps know anyone else who might be able to help me?" Don't be afraid to ask this question—the results may astonish you! Not everyone has the time or the creativity to figure out how to help you. Make it easy for them! They don't have to help you themselves—all they have to do is give you the name of someone else who can. All they have to do is pass the buck. How can someone refuse to pass the buck?

Two final tips for these network-building calls:

Call just after 5:00 PM. The long-distance rates are lower, and the person you're calling on will most likely still be there and be more relaxed and receptive than earlier in the day. Keep in mind that businesspeople are almost always busy when you call, which is fine with you: leave a message ("it's Rebecca Smith calling on a Boston College matter") and they're sure to call you back—but on their dime!

Be sure to write a thank-you letter to those who have taken the time to help you by phone or in person. It can be informal, on note paper, or a formal business letter. This is one of the best ways to impress the people who are part of your network. In fact, when your job hunt is over, it's a great idea to send a brief note to the three or four people who've been most helpful to you, telling them where you've decided to work. It's an early start on the network of your future: when you call on them for help with your next job change, they'll remember you.

Invest in Yourself

Make up your mind that your effort is going to require a financial investment. Plan now to budget $200 or more for job-hunting expenses, as shown in Figure 3. Even if making this investment means that you must take out a loan or take a part-time job, do it now—don't sacrifice your future earnings potential for want of a few hundred dollars at the start.

Figure 3

Job-Hunting Expense Budget

Expense   *Estimated Expense*

Postage

    Postcards for asking for
    Annual Reports (50) $_____

    50 initial letters   _____

    Follow-up & thank-you letters (30) _____

Stationery & supplies

    Best-quality 20# bond paper for letters
    & resumes (50 each) & interviewing
    follow-up letters (30)

    Typist service   _____

    Professional resume service   _____

Phone calls

    Follow-up to letters & interviews _____

    Arranging interviews   _____

    Network building   _____

Travel to & from information & job interviews
    (varies depending on where you live and
    want to work)   _____

Clothing for interviews (this can be your single
    biggest expense category)   _____

                      TOTAL EXPENSE $_____

Practice Makes Perfect

Experience is the name everyone
gives to their mistakes.
—Oscar Wilde

Arrange several early interviews with companies in which you are not especially interested. You'll learn the rituals of interviewing and have real-time practice in answering questions. Learning to experience the stress of interviewing is a lesson in itself. Even though you're not very interested in the firm, you'll still be nervous.

If your first choice of employer is Bank of America, don't risk having your first interview be with them. You will make mistakes—make them with Podunk Manufacturing, not B of A! When informational meetings with recruiters begin at your college, go to as many as you can. Even if you know you don't want to work in Chicago, but First Chicago Corporation holds a meeting, go and ask all of the questions about commercial banking you either feel you should, but don't, know, or because they seem inappropriate to ask in a job interview. For example, "Why would one choose commercial banking over investment banking? How much do Vice Presidents earn? How long would it take me to reach those levels? Why would someone choose First Chicago over a New York City bank? What do you look for in a candidate? What kinds of questions do you like to hear in an interview?"

The Initial Contact

In life, as in a football game,
the principle to follow is:
Hit the line hard.
—Theodore Roosevelt

Plan to send out at least fifty letters and resumes, and to conduct an intense campaign for interviews and offers in the ten firms in which you are most interested. In deciding where to send your letters, be resourceful. The Appendix lists names, addresses, telephone numbers and, in many cases, contact persons at 500 leading financial firms: commercial banks, investment banks, brokerage firms, mutual funds, and others. In addition, your Placement Office/Career Center may have lists and directories with other names and addresses. Augment these sources with the following:

1. *Moody's Bank & Finance Manual* has complete listings of all publicly-held financial firms. In virtually all business libraries and many community libraries. Most branch offices of brokerage firms have this manual and will let you use it in their office. See "Resources" at the end of this book for full bibliographic data on this and other reference manuals listed below.

2. Wiesenberger's *Investment Companies* lists mutual funds. Same availability as *Moody's*.

3. The *Money Market Directory* lists investment management firms. In business libraries. Occasionally in community libraries. If you have contacts at investment management firms, including bank trust departments, ask if they will let you use it in their office.

4. Pratt's *Guide to Venture Capital Sources* and other venture capital directories list venture capital firms. In good business libraries.

5. Read *The Wall Street Journal*. "Tombstone" ads such as the one shown in Figure 4 provide a lengthy list of investment banking firms.

6. Don't overlook the Yellow Pages as a job-hunting manual. Look under "Investment . . . ," "Financial . . . ," "Securities . . . ," and "Stock . . . ." Many successful careers have been started in small investment management or regional brokerage firms. After all, Harvard Business School doesn't want the entire first-year class to come from New York City commercial banks! Small firms may receive only a handful of job applications each year, offering you a much better chance than you would have competing with the thousands of applicants for jobs at Citibank or Merrill Lynch.

Figure 4

NEW ISSUE

May 18, 1984

$100,000,000

Wang Laboratories, Inc.

9% Convertible Subordinated Debentures due 2009

Price 100%

(Plus accrued interest from May 15, 1984.)

Copies of the Prospectus may be obtained in any State in which this announcement is circulated from only such of the undersigned or other dealers or brokers as may lawfully offer these securities in such State.

Merrill Lynch Capital Markets

Bear, Stearns & Co.	The First Boston Corporation	A. G. Becker Paribas Incorporated	Blyth Eastman Paine Webber Incorporated
Alex. Brown & Sons Incorporated	Dillon, Read & Co. Inc.	Donaldson, Lufkin & Jenrette Securities Corporation	Drexel Burnham Lambert Incorporated
Goldman, Sachs & Co.	Hambrecht & Quist Incorporated	E. F. Hutton & Company Inc.	Kidder, Peabody & Co. Incorporated
Lazard Frères & Co.	Lehman Brothers Shearson Lehman/American Express Inc.	Prudential-Bache Securities	L. F. Rothschild, Unterberg, Towbin
Salomon Brothers Inc	Smith Barney, Harris Upham & Co. Incorporated		Wertheim & Co., Inc.
Dean Witter Reynolds Inc.	McDonald & Company Securities, Inc.		Tucker, Anthony & R. L. Day, Inc.
Arnhold and S. Bleichroeder, Inc.	A. G. Edwards & Sons, Inc.		Oppenheimer & Co., Inc.
Prescott, Ball & Turben, Inc.	Thomson McKinnon Securities Inc.	Advest, Inc.	Atlantic Capital Corporation
Robert W. Baird & Co. Incorporated	Bateman Eichler, Hill Richards Incorporated		Sanford C. Bernstein & Co., Inc.
William Blair & Company	Blunt Ellis & Loewi Incorporated	J. C. Bradford & Co.	Butcher & Singer Inc.
Cable, Howse & Ragen	Cowen & Co.	Dain Bosworth Incorporated	F. Eberstadt & Co., Inc.	Eppler, Guerin & Turner, Inc.
First of Michigan Corporation	Janney Montgomery Scott Inc.		Ladenburg, Thalmann & Co. Inc.
Cyrus J. Lawrence Incorporated	Montgomery Securities		Moseley, Hallgarten, Estabrook & Weeden Inc.
Piper, Jaffray & Hopwood Incorporated	Robinson Humphrey/American Express Inc	Rotan Mosle Inc.	Rothschild Inc.
Swiss Bank Corporation International Securities Inc.	Wheat, First Securities, Inc.	Yamaichi International (America), Inc.	
Adams, Harkness & Hill, Inc.	Bacon Stifel Nicolaus Stifel, Nicolaus & Company, Incorporated		Boettcher & Company, Inc.
Brean Murray, Foster Securities Inc.	Burgess & Leith Incorporated		D. A. Davidson & Co. Incorporated
First Albany Corporation	Furman Selz Mager Dietz & Birney Incorporated		Gruntal & Co., Incorporated
Interstate Securities Corporation	Johnson, Lane, Space, Smith & Co., Inc.		Legg Mason Wood Walker Incorporated
Morgan, Keegan & Company, Inc.	Neuberger & Berman		Stephens Inc.

Banca del Gottardo	Banque Nationale de Paris	County Bank Limited
J. Henry Schroder Wagg & Co. Limited	Vereins- und Westbank Aktiengesellschaft	S. G. Warburg & Co. Ltd.

Reprinted by permission of Wang Laboratories, Inc. and Merrill Lynch Capital Markets.

Order the Annual Reports well in advance of sending your initial letter. All companies whose stock is publicly traded, whether on the New York or American Stock Exchanges or in the Over-the-Counter market, publish Annual Reports that are available to the public. These companies are listed in *Moody's Manuals*, such as *Moody's Bank & Finance Manual* described above. Even if a company is privately held, such as Dillon, Read, they may publish an annual report or review that they are happy to make available to job applicants.

Call the company and tell the switchboard operator you wish to order an Annual Report, or send a postcard asking for one. If the company is publicly held, ask also for a *proxy report*—this is a short report that is prepared each year prior to their annual meeting. It lists officers and directors, including biographical data such as ages and salaries of the highest-paid officers.

It's also a good idea to order the Annual Reports of the competitors of the companies in which you're interested. Even if you don't intend to apply to the competitor firm for a job, the data in the Annual Report will give you useful ammunition for questions to ask during your interview.

If you have no contacts in a company, direct your letter to Personnel. Make sure you have the correct name of the department (Personnel or Human Resources) and the area (Professional Recruiting or College Relations), and try to get the name of a specific person, such as the Director of College Recruiting. These names are provided for many of the firms listed in the Appendix to this book. If you don't have this information, call the company and ask for Personnel. Tell the Personnel representative that you wish to apply for a certain position and would like the name of the person to whom you should send your resume and cover letter.

It's far better to contact someone not in Personnel. Call everyone you know who may be able to give you the name of a good person to contact: an alumnus of your college, a faculty member, parent, or friend. Ask one specific question: "I'm applying for an interview with E. F. Hutton, but would like to direct my application to a specific person, not just Personnel. Can you give me the name of the proper person, or can you direct me to someone else who might help?" In most cases, the person will say, "Direct it to me."

Don't be afraid to make this phone call. You have made it as easy as possible for the people you are calling to fulfill your request quickly and painlessly. They can either handle it themselves or simply give you another person's name and send you on your way. How could anyone possibly be offended at your request? You may know of people in the company who are so far up in the hierarchy that you are uncomfortable calling on them for an information interview, but you can call on them now. If you've contacted a Senior Vice President who happens to have attended your college, you've practically guaranteed that your letter and resume will appear on the desk of the head of College Relations with the note, "George, we should talk with this young person."

Or would you rather have your letter sitting in the basket with 500 other similar requests?

> *It's easier for a letter to fall down*
> *the ladder than climb up the ladder.*
> —*Stephanie Shellman*

Regardless of whom you are writing, make sure that you have their full name (including preferred title of Mr., Ms., Mrs., or Dr., and middle initial), correctly spelled, and their title. Again, don't hesitate to ask the switchboard operator for this information.

Follow Up on Your Application

After you've sent out your letters, call the companies to determine the status of your application. For large firms, call after three weeks; for small firms, two weeks. Inquire politely: "I'm calling to check on the status of my application for a position as a Financial Analyst." It's quite possible that the letter never reached the intended recipient, or that the person mislaid it or, most likely, simply hasn't gotten around to it. Your call will be a memory- and conscience-jogger, and may initiate the action to be taken on your application.

From the day you mail your first letter until the day you get a final "yes" or "no" from the company, keep track of your application. This follow-up is sometimes the only factor separating successful job applicants from the less-successful. At any stage, your application may become bogged down; not rejected, just stuck. Gently nudge your application through the channels. At this early stage, remember that your primary objective is to get an interview. Make that the focus of all of your follow-up calls: "I'd like to know if we can arrange an interview." Don't be afraid to be persistent; as long as you are polite, and not pesky, your persistence will not harm, and will probably help, your chances of being called in for an interview.

> *Diligence is the mother of good luck.*
> *Plough deep while sluggards sleep and*
> *you shall have corn to sell and keep.*
> —Benjamin Franklin

If Your Job Hunt Is Six Months or More Away

If you are one of the fortunate few who have had the foresight to begin your job search well ahead of time, here are some tips from the pros:

1. *Take an accounting course.* Recruiters from all types of financial firms tell us that an accounting course is sometimes a requirement and always a plus. If your college doesn't offer such a course, investigate other programs in your area that might: other colleges or universities offering evening courses, community adult-education programs, even correspondence courses. If none of these is possible, there are available excellent books on accounting that you can study yourself. When your interviewers inquire whether you have studied accounting, you can answer, "yes, I have. I know how important it is to my career, and my college doesn't offer a course, so I have studied it on my own." Your interviewer will be impressed with your initiative.

2. *Make your vacations count.* If you have more summer vacation time left or a winter term that allows you to spend a few weeks working, get a job with a financial firm. Branch offices of brokerage firms are always looking for college students to help brokers prospect for new clients, and to fill in for vacationing Sales Assistants during the summer. During the school year, there are usually both paid and unpaid intern-

ships available with brokerage firms. Generally, you can work at whatever times are convenient for you: mornings, afternoons, or evenings, and work for as many hours a week as you can handle. Check the Yellow Pages for stock brokerage firm offices near you. Your Placement Office/Career Center is likely to know of other available internships. Make sure they know that you are interested.

The Buddy System

Forget your opponent.
Always play against par.
—Sam Snead

Forget about the idea that you are competing against your friends. In fact, one of the smartest things you can do is join forces with a buddy and attack the job market together. You have everything to gain from this approach:

1. You can share such expenses as ordering Annual Reports; you can also avoid the time and expense of duplicating information interviews by sharing the information;

2. You can critique each other's cover letters and resumes, and can practice answering interviewing questions;

3. You will reinforce each other when your spirits start to flag;

4. You will preserve a friendship that may otherwise become severely strained. In the long run, this may be as important to you as landing that job on Wall Street.

You have nothing to lose by helping your friend. You are different people. You may get an offer from Goldman, Sachs, while Salomon Brothers won't even interview you; your friend, on the other hand, may be snubbed by Goldman but sought-after by Salomon! Who knows why one of you will strike out at one firm and not another? Don't think about competing with your friend. Think about how the two of you are going to compete with and best thousands of other applicants from all over the country!

If At First . . .

*Success generally depends upon knowing
how long it takes to succeed.*
—Montesquieu

If you don't get a job by the time you had expected, don't worry, you are not permanently afflicted. Your job hunt will take a little longer than you had intended, that's all.

Each summer, I hear from several forlorn and bedraggled new college graduates who had somehow neglected their job hunt until too late. Often these are the Phi Beta Kappa graduates who had such confidence in their superior academic credentials that they didn't bother to really look for a job, devoting themselves instead to their honors theses and course work. As a result, they missed the hiring schedule of the commercial bank and investment bank training programs, and are convinced that they will never be able to have a career in finance.

A late start is not fatal. There are many success stories of individuals who managed to keep their spirits up and their job hunt active, were persistent and energetic, and eventually got the job of their dreams. In several of these cases, they had even been turned down once by the companies that finally hired them! The message here is obvious: don't give up!

There are plenty of jobs available for the late starter—provided that you work at it. It's true that in investment banking firms, it's extremely difficult to be hired at an entry level unless you are interviewing in the spring, about to graduate from college or business school in June. However, commercial banks differ; although some start their training programs once a year (June or July), others hire twice a year (usually for July and January), four times a year, or even continuously. Brokerage firms, mutual funds, and investment counseling firms tend to hire year-round, whenever there is a need. There are other reasons to be optimistic: a firm that rejected you in January may hire you in July. A late application may be processed because someone on whom they had counted did not start with them, after all.

It is important to be in the right place at the right time to get these jobs. That's not really difficult—just make sure that your search is continuing energetically and that you are talking with so many people at so many companies that one is just going to happen to have exactly the kind of position you had in mind.

Chapter 3

Presenting a Powerful Resume

---

*You don't have a second chance
to make a first impression.*
—*Unknown*

Cover Letters

A RESUME should never be sent without a cover letter that explains what you want and highlights what it is that is special about you. Cover letters can be even more important than resumes: first, because they're seen first; and second, because they give a better feeling for your personality. The tone of a cover letter should be natural, not too casual ("I'm checking out investment banking because I want to make a lot of money") but not too stilted ("It is my expectation that a career in investment banking will be both challenging and lucrative"). It is better to use your natural style and say something like, "I am excited by the challenge of investment banking."

In a cover letter, say:

1. Who you are;
2. What job you want;
3. What you have done that is relevant for the job
   OR one or two key points about yourself.

State what you have done, not what qualities you possess. Let the reader figure that out. Do not say:

My experience as President of College Government has developed the qualities of leadership, initiative, and the

25

ability to follow through on a project that I feel will be important in a career in commercial banking.

Instead, simply say what you have done and trust the reader to know what it means:

I am President of College Government.

Help the reader out only if what you've done is obscure. In that case, explain only what it means, not what qualities it developed or demonstrated:

In my junior year, I was elected to the Occipital Society, which consists of the top 1% of scholars in the junior and senior classes.

State specific facts about yourself. Mention the two or three things that make you special, such as:

My work experience includes summer work at Irving Bank and a small venture-capital firm, and an internship during the school year at Dean Witter.

I am an Honors candidate in Economics, preparing a thesis on "The Impact of the Strength of the U.S. Dollar on the Japanese Economy."

I have financed 40% of my college tuition and expenses while maintaining a 3.25 GPA.

One English major with a relatively low GPA by investment banking standards (3.25) had, however, mounted several entrepreneurial efforts during her college years. She mentioned them in her cover letter and got four offers from investment banks in a recent recruiting season.

Make your cover letters short, punchy, and to the point. Make sure that the most significant things about yourself are highlighted near the top of your letter. Your cover letter will probably be read in fewer than five seconds. Make sure that the reader hits the highlights before your five seconds are up!

Always end the cover letter with a statement such as, "I will contact you in a week"—and make sure that you do it. Don't assume that the reader will contact you, and don't say you'll make the contact and then not do it. When I receive a cover letter and resume, I set them aside in a pending file, waiting for the writer to call. If no call comes within the time they have indicated, I toss it. Make sure you follow up in the time you have said you would.

When you call to follow up on your letter and resume, keep in mind that your goal is to arrange an appointment for an interview.

Spell everything correctly and use proper grammar. The misspellings and grammatical errors I see on letters sent to me by some of the brightest college students in the nation never cease to amaze me. First prize goes to the letter that was addressed to me at "Meryl Lynch" (like Meryl Streep?). Then there are the perennial favorites—letters in proper business form, with the name of the writer neatly typed at the bottom of the letter—yet beginning, "Dear Ms. Calhoun, My name is John Smith . . . ." That's fine for third grade, but not for business. Don't repeat your name. Simply begin to talk about yourself:

> I am a senior at Notre Dame.

One letter from an Ivy League Honors student contained the following: " . . . grateful that Wellesley has successful alumna who are willing . . . ." Here are the rules:

> The female singular is alumna.
> The male or mixed singular is alumnus.
> The female plural is alumnae (pronounced "nee").
> The male or mixed plural is alumni (pronounced "nye").
> (note to all sharp-eyed Latin scholars: yes, the
> pronunciation of these plurals is idiosyncratic)

This same writer also lists her goals, which were "origionally" something else; her "extracirricular" activities; and offered her thesis title, "the decision of high-technology companies to compete in Communist Countries " (the rules employed for capitalization of this title elude me).

Another classic from a letter in which the writer also misspelled the name of the person who referred him to me: " . . . in regards to possibly setting up a tour of your office" (like "give my regards to Broadway!"?).

You cannot imagine what a negative impression these errors create. How can a potential employer have confidence in your ability to prepare a correct registration statement for the Securities and Exchange Commission if you cannot even spell Merrill Lynch?

If you cannot spot the errors in the above paragraphs, or if you aren't absolutely sure what they are, please, please, have a friend, faculty member or counselor from your Placement Office/Career Center edit your letters!

Resumes

Invest in decent, highest-grade bond paper and envelopes. Don't use corrasable bond; it smears. Use a heavy-weight paper like Eaton's Berkshire typewriter paper (parchment bond, heavy weight, 20 lb.).

If the burden of typing and duplicating high-quality resumes is too much for you, consider investing in a resume-preparation service. Most people who have their resume professionally printed find it well worth the expense. For one thing, they will provide the needed editing referred to above. For another, your resume will look crisp and professional. If your resume is over-long, they can also reduce it in size and cram in more data on one sheet while still retaining a neat and uncluttered appearance.

Many students are producing their resumes on word processors or computers, which is fine; it demonstrates proficiency with a computer system. Make sure, however, that your cover letter is personalized and individually typed; a word-processed cover letter tells the readers that they are not a company in which you have a particular, serious interest.

Whether your resume is computerized or hand-typed, make sure that you are using a fresh ribbon to obtain a crisp, dark look.

Study the sample resumes and cover letters shown in this chapter. There are books available with many more examples. Your Placement Office/Career Center may offer workshops on resume preparation as well as having professional staff members who can help. Here are the key points to consider on your resume:

Include all evidence of your achievements. Everyone has something that makes them special. Make sure it is obvious on your resume. Convey leadership and success. List anything that really matters to you—academic, volunteer, or political activities. If you are a superlative pianist, say so.

One commonly-overlooked area is that of part-time jobs. Perhaps you weren't on a sports team or active in other campus activities because you were putting yourself through school or working for part of your tuition? Say so! Be quite specific if you have done something extraordinary:

> Worked 20 hours per week unpaid internship during school term.

The fact that you were out working shows that you are a go-getter, a hard worker, and just the sort of person your potential employer is looking for!

Make sure you can be located. If you are a student, put both your room telephone and a dormitory telephone number on your resume to increase the chances that you can be reached. Remember that your calls will come from 9 to 5, when many students are most likely to be out of their rooms. You'll find that an answering machine will be an excellent investment. If you are working at another job and want your job-hunting activities to be confidential, indicate in your cover letter when and where you can be reached ("I can be reached by mail at the above address or by telephone after 5:30 PM at xxx-xxx-xxxx").

Omit the obvious or inappropriate: the word "resume," your health, weight, sex, marital status. Omit an objective. It should be clearly stated in your cover letter. Omit "references available upon request." Of course they are. Omit self-assessments like "good interpersonal skills." Your interviewer will figure out whether they are good or not.

Omit anything that's not really important . . . minor clubs, societies, and jobs that have no bearing on your career field. Don't hesitate to lump together summer and vacation jobs with this kind of summary:

> Summers,   Various jobs, including: lifeguard, waitress,
> 1979-1981   construction worker, soda jerk

Figure 5 — Sample Cover Letter

896 Elmwood Avenue
Hartford, CT 06115
February 16, 1985

Mr. John L. Carleton
Manager of College Recruiting
Daniels Brothers and Company, Incorporated
One New York Center
New York, NY 10000

Dear Mr. Carleton:

I will graduate from Eastern University with a Bachelor of Arts degree in Economics in June of 1985. As you will see from my resume, which is enclosed, my course work also includes Accounting studies at the Albert School of Management.

With business experience at Dean Witter, the Federal Reserve Bank of New York, and Hamilton, Muller, and O'Hara, I have decided to pursue a career in investment banking. I am particularly interested in Daniels Brothers' Financial Analyst Program.

In addition to financing 40% of my college tuition and expenses by working at many jobs during the school term and vacations. I serve as President of the Sigma Chi Fraternity and am on both the Varsity Baseball and Track Teams.

I will be in New York from March 1 through March 5, 1985, and look forward to meeting with you to discuss the benefits I could bring to Daniels Brothers as a Financial Analyst. I shall contact you shortly to arrange an appointment.

John Q. Smith

Figure 6 — Sample Resume

JOHN Q. SMITH
896 Elmwood Avenue
Hartford, CT 06115
203-xxx-xxxx

EDUCATION

1982 to present	EASTERN UNIVERSITY	Hartford, CT

EASTERN UNIVERSITY — Hartford, CT
Expect Bachelor of Arts degree in Economics, June, 1985
President, Sigma Chi Fraternity
Athletics: Varsity Baseball
Varsity Track
Financed 40% of college tuition and expenses

Fall 1983 — ALBERT SCHOOL OF MANAGEMENT — Hartford, CT
Studied Financial and Managerial Accounting

1981-1982 — WILLIAMSON COLLEGE — Arlington, VA
Recipient of Negro National Merit Scholarship
Completed freshman year; transferred to Eastern University

BUSINESS EXPERIENCE

1983 to present — DEAN WITTER — Hartford, CT
Prospect for new clients for Account Executives via telephone solicitation. Unpaid internship 10 hours per week.

Summer 1984 — FEDERAL RESERVE BANK OF NEW YORK — New York, NY
Selected as Summer Intern. Analyzed statistical data concerning foreign currencies. Presented recommendations on correlating activity in Japanese yen with U.S. monetary policy to senior economists.

Summer 1983 — HAMILTON, MULLER, AND O'HARA — Chicago, IL
Acted as Legal Assistant at this large law firm. Prepared research and attended hearings on ROA antitrust case.

Summers 1981, 1982 — Laborer, Arnold Construction Company — Chicago, IL

During school terms have worked as bartender in campus pub, store clerk, tax return preparer, babysitter, and landscape worker.

SPECIAL INTERESTS — Enjoy many sports, including baseball, tennis, and squash.

Figure 7 — Sample Cover Letter

Emory Hall
Southern University
Baton Rouge, LA 70816
January 26, 1985

Mrs. Emily H. Potter
Managing Partner
Armstrong, Hendrick, and Wood & Company
Two Montgomery Center
San Francisco, CA 94104

Dear Mrs. Potter:

Thank you for your time on the phone this morning. As you suggested, I am enclosing my resume. I will greatly appreciate your help in presenting my application for a position as Junior Financial Analyst with Armstrong, Hendrick and Wood.

As you know, I am an Honors candidate for a Bachelor of Arts degree in Political Science and Mathematics in June of 1985. My course work has included a number of courses in Economics and Computer Science, and my business experience has included a summer spent with Corestates Financial, a position that involved extensive analytical work.

My personal background includes serving as Stroke on the Southern Conference-winning Varsity Crew, and fluency in French and Spanish from years spent living abroad.

I deeply appreciate your help in arranging an interview with your firm. I will contact you in a week to discuss a mutually-convenient time. Thank you again for your assistance.

Sincerely,

Rebecca M. Smith

Figure 8 — Sample Resume

REBECCA M. SMITH

Emory Hall	1843 South Woodside Avenue
Southern University	Fairport, NY 14450
Baton Rouge, LA 70816	716-xxx-xxxx
504-xxx-xxxx or 504-xxx-xxxx	

EDUCATION

SOUTHERN UNIVERSITY
Baton Rouge, Louisiana
Honors candidate for B.A. degree, June, 1985
Major: Political Science   Minor: Mathematics
Stroke, Varsity crew (winners of 1984 Southern
Conference)
Dormitory Council
Volunteer, Inner-City Collegiate Exchange (tutored
elementary-school inner-city children)

PERTINENT COURSES

Principles of Economics (Macro and Micro)	Accounting
Computer Science (BASIC, FORTRAN)	Finance
Management Information Systems	Economic Statistics
The Banking System (Domestic and International)	

WORK EXPERIENCE

Summer   CORESTATES FINANCIAL
1984   Philadelphia, Pennsylvania

Researched and presented detailed studies on financial
planning services and personal cash management accounts. Formulated potential acquisition list. Contributed
research to studies on the affluent market, relationship
banking, and reasonable compensation for personal trust
services. Used personal computer for statistical comparisons and graphs.

Summers
1981-1983 Sailing instructor, waitress, camp counselor
Fairport, New York area

SKILLS   Fluent in French and Spanish. Knowledge of German.

ADDITIONAL INFORMATION

Born in Geneva, Switzerland. U.S. citizen. Have lived in
Geneva, Switzerland and Rio de Janeiro, Brazil.

INTERESTS   Serious interest in photography
Sailing, running, and swimming enthusiast.

Don't include any kind of description of these jobs:

> Waitress — organized thrice-daily setting of tables; planned table assignments; interfaced with customers; aided in customer decision-making; served meals to customers; supervised busing of tables; monitored level of condiment jars and bottles.

Consider listing relevant courses. For example, if you majored in a non-quantitative field such as Political Science, History, English, or Art History, but took courses in Business, Economics, Accounting, Mathematics, or Computer Science, consider listing them on your resume so that the readers will know that you have quantitative skills. It's especially important to list Accounting courses on your resume in applying for any financial job. If your quantitative courses were many, consider listing them on a separate sheet.

The one-page resume is ideal. 95% of college students' resumes fit well on one page. If they can't, it's usually because they're cluttered with trash about summer jobs or obvious/inappropriate items such as those listed above. If you've carefully edited and still overflow, consider a professional resume printing service that may be able to reduce yours to one page; if even that doesn't do the trick, you must be a real powerhouse with a lot of strong, pertinent experience. Go ahead and use a second page.

Sports! One of the most valuable things you can do for your career is to participate in sports, particularly team sports. If you have any shred of evidence of sporting activity, make sure it's on your resume. I once evaluated the resume of a young person who was one of the top three ranked tennis players in New England—and it wasn't on the resume! If you have no collegiate or team sports to display, make sure that your "Personal Interests" section includes them: tennis, skiing, running, hiking, squash, racquetball, canoeing, mountain climbing, hang gliding, golf, Nautilus, anything.

Use action verbs. Make sure that every descriptive phrase starts with an action verb such as those listed in Figure 9. Banish the term "responsibilities included" forever! Make every description short, punchy, and attention-getting.

Figure 9

Action Verbs

Initiated	Acted as liaison	Provided
Prepared	Supervised	Coordinated
Directed	Conducted	Negotiated
Completed	Coordinated	Mediated
Researched	Launched	Designed
Wrote	Started	Invented
Edited	Corrected	Studied
Implemented	Improved	Increased
Performed	Tested	Instructed
Maintained	Translated	Organized
Updated	Established	Scheduled
Volunteered	Reviewed	Examined
Formulated	Assisted	Counseled
Determined	Consulted	Served
Planned	Sold	Guided
Advised	Solved	Trained
Arranged	Promoted	Compiled
Acted	Produced	Created

Remember that a resume does not require complete disclosure. If something is trivial or unimportant, feel free to leave it out. When you complete your official application form for the job, it will ask you to "list every single job you have had in the last ten years and account for every minute of your time between jobs." Comply with full disclosure at that point, but omit the unimportant until then. This doesn't mean that you can omit something that should be included that you'd rather forget about, but it does mean that you can make sure that there will be room for everything that is really important.

Consider a skills section. Include foreign languages and computer languages. Try to express the degree of your knowledge: "fluent in Spanish; working knowledge of French and German," "have worked in COBOL, BASIC, and FORTRAN."

Sticky issues. The questions most frequently asked about resumes are those concerning discriminatory or controversial issues. Should Blacks receiving a Negro National Merit scholarship mention it on their resume? Should Jews mention their participation in Hillel activities? Similar questions arise for those who participate in feminist organizations, Republican or Democratic political activities, and even for members of MENSA (an organization for those with high IQ's).

The general rule is, anything which is truly important to you should be mentioned . . . but be very careful. It was only a few years ago that entrance to many top financial firms was blocked to Jews and Blacks. Discrimination is now mostly behind us. For Jews, today it's almost a non-issue. Blacks' minority status is much more likely to be a plus than a minus in getting hired. However, one involved in feminist activities should not mention them on a resume or in an interview. There is still too much prejudice on this subject on Wall Street. Make an impact by getting hired first, then bring about changes in attitudes by working effectively from the inside.

Political activities are almost always a plus. Don't worry about whether you and your interviewers are members of the same party. Financial companies want to hire people who are vitally interested in the world around them. They also recognize that participating in a political campaign augments your academic credentials with valuable real-world experience. I know of one instance where the resume of a MENSA member was tossed away by a major financial firm because the partner reviewing the resume was terrified that she'd be smarter than he was. I recommend not mentioning MENSA unless you know that the specific person reviewing the resume is also a MENSA member.

Ask several "pros" to review your cover letters and resumes. Faculty members, alumni, people you've contacted in your network building, Placement Office/Career Center staff . . . all will help you hone the fine details that will make yours a powerful, attention-getting, action-producing resume!

Chapter 4

Successful Interviewing: Preparation, Strategies, and Techniques

I came, I saw, I conquered.
—Julius Caesar

YOU, TOO, CAN BE A WINNER: look like a winner, act like a winner, and think like a winner—even in an interview! This chapter targets interviewing strategies to make you a winner.

First, understand that you must be in control of your interview, and that control begins with proper preparation. If you are preparing for an interview in investment banking, learn all you can about that field. Yes, it seems obvious—but why do so few applicants really do it? Recruiters from The First Boston Corporation, a top-tier investment banking firm, routinely interview students who confuse them with the First National Bank of Boston! Make sure that you're one of the smart minority of job seekers who take the time and trouble to prepare properly.

While you're sitting around fretting about whether your grade point average is high enough to get you a job with Lehman Brothers, another student with a lower average than yours is in the Placement Office/Career Center or the library reading, arranging information interviews, or sending postcards asking for Annual Reports. You may think you're preparing, but you're really only stalling. Guess which one of you is more likely to get the job?

Thorough preparation for your interviews could put you farther ahead of the crowd than a 3.8 GPA or the Presidency of College Government. Begin today to take control of your interview.

Prepare With Information

Learn as much as possible about the firms with which you'll be interviewing so that you'll be able to answer their questions and ask them good, insightful questions of your own.

1. Keep a small notebook (6″ by 9″ or smaller). During your research phase, take notes and write down questions and ideas as you think of them. When you study the sample interviewing questions in Figure 10 in this chapter, write down your answers in your notebook.

   Want to guarantee that you'll be nervous in an interview? Try to memorize the questions you want to ask. Instead, take your notebook with you so that you can refer to it if necessary for the questions you're going to ask.

   Use the notebook also to jot down names of those you meet during your interviews. After the interview, write down questions they asked and your answers. Criticize your performance in writing so that you can refer to it when preparing for your next interview.

2. Study the chapters on financial careers in this book. Their purpose is to give you an introductory explanation of the activities of various types of financial firms, and to help you decide which careers will interest you.

3. Visit your Placement Office/Career Center and read their informational books on the industry or job category, plus specific articles or clippings on the firm(s) in which you're interested.

4. Spend some time in the library reading business periodicals. Study articles on current topics of interest. For example, how Rule 415 affects investment banking, how commercial banks such as BankAmerica Corporation are acquiring discount brokerage firms such as Charles Schwab & Co., how the current bull or bear market cycle affects the financial strength of brokerage firms, and what repeal of the Glass-Steagall Act will mean to these firms. At the ends of the chapters in Part II, "Career Choices," in this book, several short articles are listed under "Sug-

gested Reading." They are in common business periodicals available in any library. Read these articles to further develop your knowledge of these fields.

5. Talk to your Business or Economics professors, particularly those who teach courses in Finance or Accounting. Ask them to suggest topics of current interest in the field and questions you can ask during your interviews.

6. Contact alumni of your college who have careers in the field. Your Placement Office/Career Center should be able to give you their names. Ask them the same questions.

7. Read the Annual Report of the company you're interviewing and the Annual Reports of their competitors. They contain valuable information about products, markets, problems, and strategies, enabling you to formulate many excellent questions.

8. Branch offices of brokerage firms can be helpful. It's better to visit them than to call (once they know you're not a potential client, they may try to get you off the phone, but will treat you politely if you walk in). Read the "S&P sheets" (Standard & Poor's *Stock Reports*—one-page writeups on public companies) and the *Value Line Investment Survey* reports on the companies in which you're interested. Most banks, insurance companies, and many brokerage firms are written up in these reports. Ask also if they have any recent research reports available on these companies. If they do, most brokerage offices will let you have them free of charge.

Strategies for Successful Interviewing

Be Prepared to Answer Questions

Each of the questions in the list in Figure 10 is an actual question recently asked by commercial or investment banking interviewers. Study the list and answer each question. Unless you are unusually articulate under pressure, write out each of your answers. Be truthful in answering, but learn to present your most favorable qualities. For example, when asked, "what is your greatest weakness?" don't answer, "I'm always late," but instead, "I sometimes take on too many commitments"! Or, think about other "weaknesses" that are really strengths, such as impatience, a trait common to many hard-working, hard-driving business people. It's also possible to thoughtfully reply that you aren't aware of any weaknesses that would affect your performance on the job.

"Tell me about yourself" is the most common question. Don't answer by beginning, "I was born in Alexandria, Virginia . . ." Do begin with something that is important to you today and work backward to include one or two other impressive things about yourself: "I'm majoring in Psychology and am writing an Honors thesis on the effect of negative feedback on extrasensory perception. I'm working part time in a psychological testing lab and also at the campus pub to earn part of my tuition money. I want to work at Drexel Burnham."

Be specific in your answers. For example, if asked "Why should we hire you?" don't say "I have drive and intelligence and am a hard worker." Say instead, "I have the kind of intelligence and drive that enabled me to earn a 3.2 GPA and still make $100 a week working part time."

Be Positive!

*No one can make you feel inferior
without your consent.*
—Eleanor Roosevelt

Be positive about everything: your skills, your college, your courses, your classmates. Be enthusiastic about these things. Be prepared to explain why you chose your college. Be prepared to defend a liberal arts education or a pre-med concentration. If you have majored in a field that doesn't seem to be directly applicable to finance, be prepared to discuss it positively. I majored in Biology in college, a field with absolutely no relevance to any job I have ever had. I'm always asked about it in interviews, and I quickly and positively present the reasons it enhances my potential in the field in which I'm interviewing: it taught me creative, analytical thinking and allowed me to develop research skills which apply to other areas.

Figure 10

50 Interviewing Questions Asked by Financial Firms

1. Tell me about yourself.

2. What is your greatest strength? Your greatest weakness?

3. Why are you interested in (investment banking)?*

4. Why are you interested in cur firm?

5. Why weren't you on a sports team?

6. Why are you leaving your major field?

7. Why did you choose your college?

8. What other companies are you interviewing with?

9. Why do you have only a B average?

10. Tell me a joke (variation: a dirty joke) or a funny story about yourself.

11. What do you think about business school? Have you taken GMATS? What was your score?

12. What do you do in your free time?

13. Do you have any questions for me?

14. What makes you think you will survive in this environment?

15. Describe yourself in three adjectives.

16. What is the most outrageous (or best or worst) thing you have ever done?

17. Why should we hire you?

18. You have one minute to impress us.

19. What's the highest position you expect to achieve in life?

20. What was the best course you took in college? The worst?

21. Looking back, what would you do differently?

Interviewing Questions — *Continued*

22. What do you think it takes to succeed in this business?

23. What is it about you that might be a disadvantage at this firm?

24. What differentiates you from your classmates?

25. What is the most important contribution you've made to your college?

26. Does your mother work? What does your father do?

27. What will you bring to us that no one else will?

28. How would your friends describe you?

29. How comfortable are you with computers?

30. Do you have a hard time saying no?

31. Do you have any other offers yet?

32. What do you dislike most about your college?

33. What book would you recommend I read?

34. What is the next book you'd like to read?

35. If you could spend an hour with anyone in the world (past or present), who would that be?

36. Have you ever lived in New York City or spent much time here?

37. What do you not look forward to if you join us?

38. Have you taken accounting? What grade did you get?

39. Where would you like to see changes (or rectify a weakness) at our firm?

40. In what area of our firm could we best use your background?

41. How would you describe your work habits?

42. What is your opinion of the deficit? How would you resolve it?

43. What drives you?

Interviewing Questions — *Continued*

44. Give me an example of your initiative.

45. What do you see yourself doing in five years, ten years?

46. What two or three things are most important to you in your career?

47. Tell me about your job last summer.

48. What major problem have you encountered? How did you deal with it?

49. Do you think that your grades are a good indication of your academic achievement?

50. SILENCE.

51. STARE.

* Parentheses denote interchangeable terms. For example, this question could also be, "Why are you interested in mutual funds?"

Be careful of making negative assumptions in areas where you don't really have enough information. For example, if asked, "why are you not interested in commercial banking?" don't reel off a laundry list of what's wrong with commercial banking. Flip your answers to the positive: "I'm more interested in being a Research Analyst because I want my work to be more directly related to the stock market than would be possible in commercial banking." Or "I'm motivated by the greater earnings potential in investment banking."

Don't be caught in an off-base negative pronouncement such as "the commercial bankers I've met don't seem to be very excited about their jobs." Remember, your interviewer's spouse may be a commercial banker.

Never critize anything in an interview, especially yourself. About to say, "I should have taken more Economics courses"? Bite your tongue. If you're asked about it, give a good explanation ("originally I was pre-med, but have changed my career direction within the last year for three reasons . . . ").

Be enthusiastic about yourself, what you have done in school, your activities and sports, your home town, your favorite book. An enthusiastic person is one who's going to be a self-starting, motivated employee six months from now when the spirit of the troops is flagging. An enthusiastic person is not going to require hours of the manager's time spent in motivational therapy. An enthusiastic person is going to be on time and on the beam . . . in short, the kind of person your interviewer wants to have on the team, exactly the person they need. Enthusiasm is your most saleable asset!

Practice!

Practice yourself, for heaven's sake,
in little things; and thence
proceed to greater.
    —*Epictetus*

Few of those events in life in which we engage voluntarily are as stressful as a job interview. Deal with the fear which causes the stress by anticipating it and practicing how to deal with it .

Find out whether your Placement Office/Career Center will videotape you in a mock interview. It's painful and embarrassing but can be one of the most valuable steps you take in your program to get the job you want.

If your heart is set on Chemical Bank, don't let their interview be your first. Arrange early interviews with other companies in which you are not especially interested. Use your vacations to practice interviewing with any firm you can find for any professional entry-level position. Learn to experience the stress and uncertainty of interviewing, and to answer their questions. Practice with them, not with Chemical Bank. Don't feel guilty about taking advantage of them . . . after all, you are giving them a chance to offer you something irresistible. Prepare for the interview just as though they were your first choice—learn about them in advance, and practice the strategies we've outlined in this chapter.

Learning to interview is not that different from learning a sport. Both require practice, and in both you'll make some mistakes as a beginner. Make those mistakes on the practice field where it doesn't matter . . . don't drop the ball in the big game!

Sell Yourself!

Sometimes individuals, especially women, are so afraid of appearing to be egotistical that they are reluctant to sell theselves in an interview. Think of the result that this has on your interviewer, who cannot help but ask, "he presumably thinks that hiring him is a good idea—yet he's reluctant to sell me on this idea. How can I expect him to be enthusiastic about selling our services to our clients?"

You may not think of your career as a loan officer in a commercial bank, or as a securities analyst for a brokerage firm, as a career in sales. Yet the selling function is a vital component of these and almost all other financial jobs. Each time you talk to a client of the firm, you are, by representing your company, selling their services. In many cases, the client or prospect's decision on where they will do business depends on how they feel about you—after all, the services they will receive from the bank down the street are quite similar to yours. What makes the difference is you, their representative.

In order to sell yourself, come to your interview prepared with a knowledge of your strengths and examples that support them. Offer as many specific examples as you can. When I was interviewing to become a stockbroker trainee in 1975, the Sales Manager said he was reluctant to hire me because I had no sales experience. "But I have!" I insisted. "When our high school choir had a candy drive to raise money, I sold 54 dozen boxes of candy just so that I could win first prize!" He was impressed and hired me. What impressed him was not so much my sales ability but the drive that had enabled me to work to win that prize and that, he foresaw, would enable me to work hard enough to become a successful stockbroker. Without my willingness to sell myself by giving him the information about my strengths, he never would have hired me. Study the list of sample questions in Figure 10 to help you prepare to sell yourself.

Selling skills can be soft and low-key; they don't have to be hard and direct. Often good salesmanship is simply good listening and thoughtful response. It's possible to say some pretty aggressive things in a selling situation but not have them come across as aggressive because of the way you say them. Recently, a young man interviewing for a position as a Financial Analyst at one of the top investment banks was turned down as "too aggressive." In later interviews, he continued to confidently present his strengths, but did so in a softer, quieter voice.

When the time comes for you to say some pretty bold and positive things about yourself, try saying them in a soft, low, but quietly confident voice. Practice answering questions such as "Why should we hire you?" quietly and confidently.

Remember why your interviewer cares about your ability to present and support all of the reasons you are the best person for them to hire, and you'll find that selling yourself in your interview will be a lot more comfortable than you may have thought. Your interviewer will note how well you present the reasons you're the best person for the job and will make the connection that you'll be able to represent the company in the same effective way.

Understand What the Interviewer Really Wants

What does your interviewer really want? The answer is not obvious to most interviewees: the interviewer wants to hire you. She hasn't taken time out of her busy day to talk with someone who isn't right for the job, but with someone who she hopes will work out . . . in fact, she may hope that you'll be hired even more than you do! Why does she have this amazing point of view? Because what she wants most of all is to stop recruiting and interviewing and get back to work.

Thus, your job in an interview is simply to confirm what the interviewer hopes and you already know: that you are indeed the right person for the job.

Think also about what type of person the recruiter or interviewer is looking for. Wall Street firms generally want people who are incredibly hard-working, because they want to make sure that they'll be able to handle the grueling hours that most of these jobs require. They usually look carefully at grades, believing that good grades indicate that the person is a hard worker. If your grades aren't outstanding, don't just assume you can't get the job. Think about why they are looking at grades . . . that they are looking for a hard worker . . . and find the parts of your background that demonstrate that you are a hard worker. Then make sure that you let them know during your interview that this is true.

It may be difficult to analyze what kind of person they really want. For example, one might characterize investment bankers as aggressive, hard-driving individuals. But remember that, if you're interviewing for the position of Financial Analyst, you're at the bottom of the ladder. You're not yet an investment banker, you're an investment banker's go-fer. You are not going to be sent straight out to develop new business, but you will be sent to the firm's library to spend many midnight hours gathering data that will make the higher-ups on your team look good. Although some investment banking firms do hire the aggressive, hard-driving types as Financial Analysts, others seem to seek out the quieter, more studious sorts who will be dutiful drudges for the VP's. Try to find a happy medium: demonstrate poise and grace under fire with a self-assured yet studious attitude that will let them know that you're interested in developing and enhancing business for the firm, but that you understand completely what your responsibilities include . . . evenings spent in the library are a vital part of your work and are necessary to get the team's job done.

Wall Street firms also want someone who is articulate, poised, and intelligent. Find these qualities in yourself, then practice presenting them in an interview situation. Practice answering the sample questions by yourself, with a friend, in front of the mirror, with a tape recorder, walking to class, in your head, in your car, but practice! Expect to be questioned about anything on your resume, and practice answering those questions. As you work on your answers to the questions, write them down. Few of us are as articulate under stress as we are when at leisure, and writing down your questions in advance will help you become so familiar with them that you'll be able to answer them eloquently even under the stress of an interview.

Financial firms want to hire people who are prepared—people who will impress clients and prospects with their preparation and knowledge. Successful businesspeople don't "wing it" for important presentations; neither should you. Demonstrate this quality by being well-prepared for your interview.

Make Your Interviewer Look Good

Some interviewers' number one goal is to present their superiors with someone of whom they will approve and thus win praise for themselves. Think hard about how you can help make it easy for your interviewer to recommend that you be hired. Could he tell someone that you're recommended because you're attractive? Of course not, even though that may, in fact, be a reason—both male and female financial professionals tend to be good-looking. Help the interviewer find objective reasons: "I hired her because she was extremely well-prepared, knew our industry and company, and asked excellent questions." With proper preparation, you can guarantee that your interviewer will offer these objective reasons about you. Your interviewer will use these reasons to justify other, subjective feelings: "I feel she will be able to work well with others." Give the interviewer the ammunition—the objective reasons—to persuade others to hire you!

Get the Interviewers to Talk about Themselves

Think about the last time you met a new person you really enjoyed . . . business or social, male or female. Then think about why you enjoyed yourself so much. Chances are it's because you did most of the talking. The other person probably seemed so interested in you that he asked you questions and gave you a chance to talk about yourself. You probably ended up thinking that the other person really liked you. He would have liked you a lot better had you been asking him about himself and allowed him to do the talking!

This is a reality of human nature, one that applies equally to social intercourse and to interviewing: people like to talk about themselves. Want to make another person like you? Don't talk about yourself; don't tell her how clever you are or about the time you sailed in the South Pacific or how you got a Fulbright. Ask her about herself.

In your interview, ask your interviewer at least one personal question. Some classics are:

— tell me about your job;

— how did you get to be where you are?

— have you ever regretted your decision to become a (securities analyst)?

— do you have an MBA? How important is having an MBA in this field?

— where do you see yourself in ten years?

— what suggestions do you have for someone just beginning a career in (investment banking)?

If you're in luck, your interviewers will happily talk about themselves and end up really liking you!

Match Your Questions to the Interviewer

Be careful, though, to ask questions appropriate to the interviewer's position in the firm. If the interviewer is in Personnel, your questions will be different from those you would ask of a Vice President. For example, "how did you get to be where you are?" is inappropriate if the interviewer hasn't gotten anywhere. If you ask Personnel people their opinion of the proposed repeal of the Glass-Steagall Act, it will appear too artificial. Ask the Personnel people solid questions about the firm such as those listed in Figure 11, "Questions You Can Ask in an Interview," but ask the "Industry Issues" questions of the VP's.

Figure 11

Questions You Can Ask in an Interview

1. During the training period, how much exposure is there to different areas of the firm?

2. How much of the training program is in a classroom, and how much is on the job?

3. After the training period, how much choice does one have in the area to which one is assigned?

4. What percentage of your trainees leave at the completion of the training program? After one year? Five years? Why do they leave?

5. How much client contact do first- and second-year people have?

6. How much traveling do they do?

7. How long does it typically take to make Vice President? Partner?

8. How does this firm differ from (another in the same industry)?

9. How important is having an MBA degree to success at this firm?

10. What do you feel are the key reasons an individual would choose this firm over your competitors?

11. To your clients, what advantages do you offer over your competitors?

12. What do you like best about this company? Least?

Ask Questions about These Industry Issues

1. Increased competition among financial supermarkets.

2. Rule 415 (Shelf Registration).

3. Possible repeal of the Glass-Steagall Act.

4. Consolidation of investment banking firms.

5. Consolidation of financial and consumer services firms.

6. Competition for full-service securities brokerage firms from discount brokers.

7. Importance to securities brokerage firms of retail vs. institutional or corporate business.

8. What future changes will have the greatest impact on the securities industry?

9. What is the greatest challenge your firm will face in the next five years?

See "Suggested Reading" at the ends of chapters in Part II of this book, "Career Choices." Short articles that discuss these issues are listed. All are in easily-obtained business periodicals.

The Pressure Interview

Success depends on previous preparation,
and without such preparation
there is sure to be failure.
—Confucius

Certain companies, particularly investment banking houses, are famous for giving pressure interviews. The object here is to break down or wear out applicants and force them to show their true colors. The pressure ranges from a badgering or intimidating attitude on the part of the interviewer ("what makes you think you're tough enough to be an investment banker?") to extremes such as asking you to open a window that has been nailed shut.

Stay cool, stay confident, and don't lose your head. Perhaps you will be shown into a small room, introduced briefly to three grim-looking people, and told, "you have one minute to impress us." If you have adequately prepared for the interview, then you have practiced discussing your strengths and accomplishments and can present them briefly and clearly. The more you have practiced, the calmer you'll be.

You may be asked questions that are discriminatory and are, in fact, illegal. Pointing that out will only ensure that you won't be hired. Try to answer questions such as "are you planning on having children?" briefly and noncommittally, then change the subject. If you're asked something that's really out of line (the days of a woman being asked what form of birth control she is using are behind us, but it's not unheard-of for interviewers to ask a woman why she needs to work, when her husband has a job), answer, pleasantly but firmly, "I don't think that's really an issue here," and change the subject.

Remember, also, that you are not in a court of law under oath, and will not be jailed for contempt if you refuse, graciously and confidently, to answer any question. For example, you might be asked to criticize specific classmates who are also interviewing with the firm, or asked why the company should hire you instead of them. If you're not comfortable with this, it's okay to say, "I know that my own strengths are drive, intelligence, and the ability to communicate well with others. I don't know if they share these qualities or not."

The all-day interview represents yet another type of pressure. Here the object is simply to see if you can hold up when you're physically and mentally tired.

> *If thou faint in the day of adversity,*
> *thy strength is small.*
> —*Proverbs 24:10*

After your career is launched, and you are caught up in a heavy schedule of traveling and calling on clients, you will be required to be at your brightest and best at all times. You may have landed in Newark at 7:00 A.M. after departing San Francisco at 10:00 P.M. on the "Red-eye," and be expected to make an important presentation to a client at 9:00 A.M.—two hours after your arrival on this crowded all-night flight.

An all-day interview is testing your stamina, to see whether you have the endurance for such long business days. During the course of your interview you may spend time with as many as ten or twelve people, including several who have so little to say that you'll be exhausted just trying to keep the conversation moving. Remember that they're trying to find out how well you will conduct yourself with their clients. On a long, lengthy, and incredibly boring plant tour, will you be able to keep asking intelligent questions about the business? Prove it by coming up with plenty of questions to ask of your interviewers. These are occasions on which your classic questions such as "how did you get your job?" can be invaluable.

Lunch is usually a key part of the all-day interview, and you may be subject to intense pressure to join in the drinking. Chances are that this, too, is intentional. If you can really hold your liquor and most of your hosts are drinking, have one drink or one glass of wine. But the non-alcoholic choices of Perrier, cranberry juice, "Virgin Mary" (a "Bloody Mary" without the vodka), or the all-time Wall Street favorite, iced tea, are perfectly acceptable. Don't be tempted to order a drink unless you are absolutely sure it won't affect you.

At the end of your interviewing day, you may be invited to the local pub "for a few pops." You will be tempted to relax, bask in your delight that it's over, and hoist a few with your new-found friends. Don't, unless you are positive you can handle it; if you do, be careful. If you can drink, this is a better time and place than lunch. Remember that they are trying to get you to let down your guard for a very real business reason: they want to see how you will act with their clients. After a long and grueling day of travel, presentations, and meetings, ended by joining your clients for a drink, are you going to undo the day's delicate negotiations with your careless and now somewhat thick tongue? Or can you be relied upon to keep a cool head at all times? If you can, there's no harm in showing them, with one or two drinks. If you can't, or if you haven't had enough drinking experience to know whether you can or not, simply don't. Retaining control over your faculties is the way to keep control in this situation. If they pressure you to the point where you're uncomfortable, ask yourself whether you really want to launch your career with a group to whom drinking is so important.

Just remember that loose lips sink ships—a favorite Wall Street motto. Make sure they understand, whether you join in the drinking or not, that they won't have that problem with you on their side!

> *If A equals success, the formula is*
> *A = X + Y + Z. X is work. Y is play.*
> *Z is keeping your mouth shut.*
> *—Albert Einstein*

Prepare for the Worst

Psychological studies have shown that one of the key characteristics of successful executives is their preparation for making important decisions and taking significant risks. Typically, they first determine the worst thing that can happen if they take a particular course. Then they figure out whether they can live with that result. If the answer is yes, they proceed to make the decision and take the risk with confidence because they already know that they are prepared to handle the worst possible outcome. Less-successful executives tend to fail to take this all-important step.

Adapt this attitude to your advantage in interviewing. Plan in advance for the worst possible things that can happen, and then think about how you can prevent them from happening or, if they happen anyway, how you will handle them. In your mind, picture something awful happening to you, and then picture yourself handling it with dignity.

What are some of the worst things that could happen to you in an interview? Your nose could start to run, or you could find yourself frustrated and embarrassed because you haven't prepared adequately for your interview, and an intimidating interviewer could make you want to cry. Prevention of these problems is easy. Always carry a handkerchief or tissue in your pocket, and follow the preparation steps outlined in this book.

Probably the most common fear we have in interviews is that of being asked a question to which we don't know the answer. Picture yourself being asked, "why are you interested in Alex. Brown rather than L. F. Rothschild?" when you haven't a very good idea of what their differences are. It's okay—don't panic—simply react as you have programmed yourself in advance. Answer the question if you have an answer; otherwise say, "actually, I'm also considering L. F. Rothschild, and am still collecting information in order to compare the two firms. Perhaps you could tell me how you see the differences." Or, "that's the kind of distinction I find it most difficult to find out about, as there's not much in print. Perhaps you could tell me . . . ."

If your interviewer is really mean, nasty, and intimidating, just ask yourself whether you really want to work with this person anyway. Remember, your goal is to picture yourself handling every circumstance with dignity. The dignity in this situation comes from realizing that the interviewer is a jerk, and if that attitude is representative of others in the company, you don't want to work for them. If you leave the interview with the attitude, "they'd have to beg me to come and work for them," you can consider it a success.

> *Nothing in life is so exhilarating*
> *as to be shot at without result.*
> *—Winston Churchill*

Visualize yourself at your confident best, handling with dignity any question or challenge thrown at you. Remember, if you have prepared adequately for your interview, there is no reason to be embarrassed if you do not know the answer to any of their questions. It's always okay to say, "that's an interesting question . . . I haven't come across that issue in my reading."

Silence Is Golden

An effective technique in any business discussion, including an interview, is silence. Many interviewers will, at some point during the interview, simply stop talking. Almost all of us are tempted to dive into the uncomfortable silence and fill the void with words. Usually the words we throw in are just babble . . . more unwanted and unnecessary information about the last topic discussed or a tangential bit of personal information of no interest to anybody. Be aware that this will happen in your interviews.

Practice with a friend. When silence strikes, learn to be comfortable with it. Try to learn to use the silence to gather your own thoughts and then, if you must speak, ask one of your prepared questions. If you find yourself mind- and tongue-tied, simply turn calmly to your notebook which is close at hand, and ask your question. Again, you can see the importance of writing down your questions. In fact, the confidence of knowing that they are there if needed will probably prevent you from freezing and forgetting them, but they are there if you suddenly find your mind a blank. Simply glance at your notes and calmly ask, "do you think the trend toward consolidation of investment banking firms will continue?"

Interviewing Is a Two-Way Street

Remember that interviewing is a two-way street. It's their job to help you understand why Bankers Trust offers you the best opportunities, just as it is yours to help them understand why you're the best person for the job.

Try this mental trick as a last-minute confidence booster: just before you go in the door for your interview, think, "I'm interviewing them." You'll be surprised at the difference it can make in your confidence and poise.

Visualize the Winner . . . You!

Put the finishing touch on your interview preparation by endowing yourself with a positive, winning attitude. Visualize yourself working for this firm, in this job. See yourself walking down the streets of the financial district heading for your job, a bright, hard-working, articulate, confident Analyst in Corporate Finance. Think about how fortunate you are that you have the talent to be successful in the world of finance. Think about how excellent your education has been, and how valuable your strengths and skills are. Now head for your interview. Your positive frame of mind, your glow of inner confidence, your winning attitude will captivate your interviewer.

Last Rites, or Details Make A Difference

One More Time . . . Dressing for Successful Interviewing

> It is only the shallow people
> who do not judge by appearances.
> —Oscar Wilde

Do You Really Need a Briefcase?

Psychologically, a briefcase puts you at a disadvantage. Bending down to open it and fumbling in it are awkward acts that will disturb the momentum of your conversation and place you in a literally subordinate position. It is a cumbersome appendage. When traveling around the company or heading down the street to lunch or to visit another facility, what do you do with it? Everyone else has their hands in their pockets. Unless you have a compelling reason for carrying a briefcase, such as being required to carry examples of your work, don't do it. Carry a briefcase once you start your job, but not during an interview.

You will need to bring extra copies of your resume, your notebook or list of questions, and paper or index cards on which to take notes. In most cases, inside pockets of men's suits are adequate—even resumes can be folded and kept in a pocket. Women may be able to carry them in their pocketbook.

During the interview, you may collect descriptive material about the company that is awkward to carry about. In most cases, a manila folder will serve well. I always carry such a folder on important corporate business calls. On one side, staple in your list of questions; on the other, staple in blank paper for your own notes. This serves two purposes: one, they won't fall out;

and two, when you hand over copies of your resume to your interviewers, you won't give them your list of questions by mistake.

Some advisors on business dressing advise women not to carry a pocketbook. We are told that businessmen have difficulty with businesswomen's pocketbooks, feeling that they are unbusinesslike. For interviews to which you must travel, however, it's difficult for a woman, lacking the deep, concealed pockets so conveniently built into a man's suit, to store plane ticket, cash, credit cards, keys, and even the most minimal makeup—comb, lipstick, and mirror. Certainly it's never a good idea to carry both a briefcase and a pocketbook. Forced to choose between the two, I recommend the pocketbook. Minimize any difficulty by making sure that yours is small and unobtrusive, and don't access it in public unless it's an emergency. Place the pen you will need to take notes in your pocket or in the manila folder, hooked over the edge. Place your handkerchief or tissue in your pocket, and you and everyone else should be able to ignore the fact that you're carrying a pocketbook.

Suiting Up - for Men

This is a short discussion: first, because I don't pretend to have unique insights on the subject and refer you to those who do (John Molloy's *Dress for Success* or Michael Korda's *Success!*); second, because men's clothes are simpler than women's, and third, because men generally have a good instinctive understanding of proper business interviewing attire: dark suit in a cotton or wool blend, depending on time of year; white 100% cotton shirt, conservative tie. Wear the most expensive yet conservative clothing you can afford. If you can handle Brooks Brothers or their equivalent, do it. Don't waste your money on stylish European cuts . . . they've never made it to Wall Street.

There is still a scarcity of beards in the financial world, although mustaches are becoming more common. Even if your beard is really important to you, shave it off and grow it back after you're hired.

Dressing Up - for Women

Women should look businesslike, but feminine. Today it's hardly necessary to advise you to wear a skirt, not pants. You don't have to wear a suit; today a long-sleeved silk or silk-look-alike dress in a conservative style and color is equally acceptable. A dress may even offer you an advantage: you may be remembered as "the one in the blue dress," rather than as "one of the ten in the navy blue suits"! If you've worn a suit for your first interview, a dress may enhance your more relaxed and confident manner on a second interview.

If you are going to buy a suit for interviewing, it doesn't have to be navy blue. In fall and winter, it could be a conservative menswear shade of gray, black, or brown, or the more feminine shades of deep teal blue, dark green, or burgundy. In spring you'll have quite a bit more flexibility in color, but you should still avoid the reds, pinks, and yellows in favor of the more conservative earth tones. An exception is the blues: light blue seersucker, a popular menswear summer fabric, is acceptable.

You can see that there is a fine line to be drawn between appropriate emulation of menswear styles and fabrics and actually copying the men's attire. Menswear colors and patterns are fine, with the exception of pin stripes, a look which is simply too masculine. Please don't wear a tie—that's a direct masculine challenge, and your purpose is not to challenge, but to complement.

Men like to do business with women. They admire the qualities a good businesswoman brings to the table, and they enjoy working with her as much or more as they enjoy working with their male colleagues. Don't fight it, and don't confuse it with sexism. Men enjoy women as women enjoy men, as business colleagues and friends. Don't confuse the issue by dressing up in men's clothes . . . you may be diluting a pleasant advantage!

Try to wear a suit cut more softly than a man's. Chanel styles and unconstructed jackets are both feminine and elegant. For warm weather, the cotton-linen unconstructed styles are most comfortable but wrinkle fiercely and should be avoided. A smashing, feminine but conservative blouse, such as one with a self-bow, is a nice alternative to the collegiate look (an Oxford cloth shirt with a little grosgrain ribbon tie).

It goes without saying that plunging necklines and skirts with any sort of slit at all are unacceptable. It is impossible to sit down in a wraparound skirt without either displaying a lot of leg or holding on to the skirt. Don't wear dangly or too much or noisy jewelry. Earrings and either a necklace or a pin are fine. Pearls are a lovely, feminine, old-fashioned touch and soften a conservative suit.

Don't be too flamboyant with style or color . . . this is Wall Street, not Madison Avenue. But don't be petrified of it, either. Color experts tell us that red can be a difficult color because it tends to draw the observer's eye away from our faces. The experts also say that men dislike purple, a color most women like. When in sartorial doubt, always choose the conservative alternative.

Don't assume that colored stockings are taboo. Tina Sutton, Fashion Editor of *Savvy*, tells us that sheer hose in subdued tones coordinating with your outfit can enhance your businesslike look. For example, matching a gray skirt with gray stockings and gray or black shoes is an attractive and appropriate style for businesswomen. Navy, black, brown or taupe and, for spring through summer, bone are also acceptable. Avoid white shoes-white stockings, however, and all shades of blue (other than navy), green, lilac, purple, or burgundy.

Some male advisors on business dressing have advised women to wear hats. Don't—unless it's raining, snowing, or freezing. Women's hats do not connote business to most financial men; they conjure up the Easter Parade.

Wear low or medium heels for two reasons: one, your interviewers may be short, and it's not good politics to tower over them; second, you may have to do far more walking than you ever dreamed. Several books offering career dressing advice warn against open-toed shoes; I disagree. Tasteful open-toed shoes that complement your businesslike attire are today quite acceptable. I would, however, draw the line at ankle straps.

In rainy or snowy weather, don't sacrifice your $60 or $90 shoes by wearing them to your interview. Wear suitable "trudgies" through the elements, carry your good shoes in a bag, change in the lobby, and ask the receptionist (who is usually a fine ally in such situations) where you can unobtrusively stash your bag and shoes during the interview.

Don't be afraid to wear the same outfit to a second interview. They don't expect you to be rich, but they do expect you to dress appropriately.

Avoid the little-girl look. If your hair is long, put it up. You're kidding yourself if you think a "take me as I am" attitude makes sense. They may not really care how you wear your hair, but they care a great deal about the judgment you display—and the Alice-in-Wonderland look is an indication of poor business judgment. Remember that they're always asking themselves, "what will my clients think of her?" White stockings and dark shoes may be currently fashionable, but it's a little-girl look that is not businesslike.

The question of nail polish is interesting. Well over 50% of successful New York City Wall Street women I have met sport long, beautifully-manicured, brightly-painted nails. This is not the case in other cities. Many men still have strong prejudices against dark nail polish, and I would therefore advise caution. If you cannot live without polished nails, go ahead—but only in New York City, where businesspeople are presumably used to the idea of successful women with Nails. Everywhere else, paint if you must but use shades that are close to natural.

Perfume should be smelled only by those who come very close to you. This should not include your interviewers. It should not announce your arrival, nor should it be evident to those unfortunate enough to ride with you in an elevator. If your interviewer can smell your perfume, it's too strong. Have a friend do a sniff check before you depart for your interview.

Seven Final Tips . . . or, Don't Blow It Now!

Be on time. Plan to arrive at your destination a full 30 minutes early. Allow for unexpected traffic jams, public transportation snafus, or difficulties in finding a parking place. No matter what excuse you have for being late, it won't be good enough. The extra time will allow you to review your notes and questions, and ensure that your winning frame of mind is in place.

Learn to shake hands. I am constantly amazed that, just when I thought everyone knew the importance of a good, firm handshake, I still meet limp-wristed jobhunters—both male and female! Although occasionally I meet a real bone-crusher, with three out of ten it's like shaking hands with a lump of bread dough—lifeless and clammy. Your grip should be firm but relaxed, like holding a tennis racket while waiting to return a serve. Practice shaking hands with your friends; it's an easy knack to learn.

Look people in the eye. Many interviews have been wasted because the candidate didn't look at the interviewer! If you have this bad habit, you probably don't know it, although your friends do. It merely takes self-awareness to correct. Practice looking your friends in the eye when you talk—and make a pact with them to remind you when you're not doing it. Even more difficult is to make sure that you don't have a nervous smile or laugh. Again, if you do, you probably are not aware of it. A tendency to smile or laugh inappropriately (a trait of Jimmy Carter's) can be fatal to a listener's opinion of you. Most often, it's a self-deprecating laugh. When asked in an interview about your greatest weakness, a contemplative smile may be appropriate, but a laugh is not: "I sometimes procrastinate too much—chuckle, chuckle." That's not funny! Mock interviews with your friends, tape-recorded, if possible, can help you become aware of this unfortunate mannerism. Once aware, with some diligence on your and your friends' part, you can correct it.

Don't drink, smoke, chew, or eat during an interview. Don't chew gum. If offered coffee or something to drink or eat, decline. There is a momentum in an interview—a certain rhythm in, first, the initial handshakes and greetings and, second, the questions and answers. Devote all of your concentration to going with the flow, to maintaining the momentum of your interview. Stopping to pick up and sip coffee or eat a doughnut breaks the momentum. At lunch, order something that's easy to eat and fast to chew and swallow. Don't worry about whether it's a power selection or not—if you are asked a question after you've just taken a bite of steak or salad, you'll have to keep everyone waiting while you execute the I'll-answer-in-a-minute-as-soon-as-I-finish-this-mouthful pantomime. Fish, on the other hand, can practically be gummed—ideal for maintaining the momentum during an interview lunch.

Don't smoke, even if your interviewer does. If your interviewer is a non-smoker, you will create an instant strongly negative reaction that will be very hard to overcome. Why risk years of study and months of preparation for the fleeting pleasure of just one smoke? After you're hired, you can probably smoke a cigar at your desk if you like (after all, this is Wall Street, and some things never change)—but wait to light up until then.

Don't let down your guard. Keep up your professional demeanor in front of everybody you meet. You may be tempted to relax with a "peer flunkie," a first-year person assigned to show you around. Don't be so relieved at finding someone to confide in that you blow your friendly but cool professional manner.

Get the correct name of every person you meet. If memorizing names is too difficult for you, write them down in your notes or notebook as you go along. People are impressed if you repeat their name when they're introduced, and are happy to spell it out for you. Nothing irritates people more than seeing their name misspelled. Don't risk this mistake when you write your follow-up letters.

Even better, ask each person you meet for their card. Tuck it away in your notebook or in a pocket for later reference. Emulate the Japanese who, when given the business card of another, study it carefully for a long moment before putting it away. It honors the giver of the card, and will add to their favorable impression of you. If, after your interview, you aren't sure about the correct spelling of a name, or aren't sure whether their title is "Mr.," "Dr.," "Ms.," "Mrs.," or "Miss," or if you don't have their middle initial, be sure to call the switchboard operator for the information.

Finally we're ready for the last, vital step in your program for taking control of your interview. This is the step most often overlooked by job hunters, and one of the most important.

Follow Up On Your Interview

It's not over till it's over.
—*Yogi Berra*

Write a Follow-up Letter

Nothing impresses an interviewer more—and it is amazing how few applicants bother to do it! Send the letter the same day as your interview, if possible—hiring decisions can be made quickly. Write a formal, typed letter to your primary interviewer(s). An informal note is acceptable for someone you met briefly. "Informal" means typed or handwritten, on notepaper either plain or printed with your name and address; no flowers, kittens, or rainbows, please. Be sure to write also to the person who helped you get the interview in the first place—the on-campus recruiter, the alum whom you contacted initially, or any other individual who was especially helpful to you. They will be asked for their opinion of you as a candidate, and a fresh thank-you note or letter from you will be an important, pleasant stimulus for a good recommendation.

In all follow-up letters, reference the date and reason you met ("thank you again for the time we spent during my interview for the Loan Officer Development Program on Wednesday, January 12th."). If you are confident that you are on a first-name basis, use "Dear Marcia." If there is any question, use their title ("Dear Ms. Jones"). Reference something that will help them remember you and your conversation ("your discussion of increased pressure on fund managers for performance was especially interesting"). If someone really went out of their way to be helpful to you, say so. They probably don't do it for everybody, and it means a lot to them to know that you appreciate their generosity.

Remember to write follow-up letters to those you meet or talk with during information interviews or as part of your network-building, as well. When I organize career tours for college students in New York City and Boston, I keep notes of the names of students who take the time to send me a thank-you note or letter. When a job opening comes to my attention, those notes are the first place I look.

Find Out Why You Are Turned Down

> I do not resent criticism, even when,
> for the sake of emphasis,
> it parts for the time with reality.
> —Winston Churchill

This is one of the toughest things you will have to do in your job hunt, but one of the most important. You'll have many reasons not to find out why you were turned down:

— I already know why I was turned down;

— It's a toll call;

— I don't think I'm really interested in brokerage firms anyway;

— I'm too busy;

— they won't tell me anyway.

It's imperative that you push these reasons aside and make the call. If your interview was part of on-campus recruiting, you should be able to find out from your Placement Office/Career Center counselors. If not, call your interviewer. You may have been turned down because they didn't have any openings which were a perfect fit for you, or because, even though they liked you, they had more qualified applicants than they could hire.

Or you may be given a reason that will enlighten or astonish you. Women may be turned down because they are "too much of a feminist" or because "they came on too strongly." Men may be turned down for being "too arrogant—thinks he should be President of the company by next year—don't think he'd work well in a team." The person you are asking may not be perfectly frank with you, but will probably at least come close enough to the truth to be helpful.

There are cases where a firm was so impressed that a candidate came back to ask the reasons for rejection that they changed their minds and offered the person a job. Your own results may be less dramatic, but at least you will give yourself a chance to save your next interview by finding out what you did wrong in the last.

Think about what is most important to you: finding the job you want. Calling up to find out why you were rejected seems to be demoralizing and degrading, but it is not if it ultimately helps you get what you want.

As always, do a worst-case analysis: what is the worst thing that can happen when you make that phone call? They may tell you something negative about yourself that you don't want to hear but that you can correct and thereby enable yourself to land the Wall Street job you want.

If You Don't Hear, Follow Up

Wait two weeks after your interview, then call and politely inquire. If your "no-hear" is really a "no," you're better off knowing it now so that you can direct your efforts elsewhere. Some firms may be impressed that you have taken the trouble to follow up, and your chances may improve because of it.

One Final Word On Interviewing

The price of success is perseverance.
The price of failure comes cheaper.
—Robert Half

Whatever happens, don't lose your sense of humor. Finding a friend with whom to share the truth after a tough interview is the best way to preserve your sanity and keep your spirits up.

Understand that you are probably going to have one bad interview. But you are going to be brilliant in others and be exactly what they are looking for. When you have that bad interview, don't despair. Breathe a sigh of relief because it's behind you, and know that from now on you can look forward to nothing but terrific interviews!

Keep your winning attitude intact throughout your job search. If it flags, just visualize yourself once again in your long-awaited career . . . making an important presentation to a client, landing that elusive deal, getting your first big bonus check, and making your impact—the impact of a winner—on Wall Street.

Part II

Career Choices: Charting Your Future In Finance

Chapter 5

Evolution in Financial Services

If you do not think about the future
you cannot have one.
—John Galsworthy

IT'S PRACTICALLY IMPOSSIBLE to find a Wall Street career that is not fast-paced and challenging, exhilarating and exhausting. Research analysts and portfolio managers testify to a lifelong fascination with the stock market. Investment bankers who put in eighty-hour workweeks are obviously sincere when they tell new recruits that they do it because it's fun. Trainees in commercial bank training programs often find the regimen both more rigorous and more stimulating than they had expected.

There are differences in the types of personalities of individuals attracted to different fields and differences in the lifestyle options offered by their careers. Some present the lifetime prospect of sixty-to-eighty-hour workweeks, while others eventually settle into eight-hour days. Different careers offer different compensation—from the prosaic five-figure salaries earned by some portfolio managers to the fabled megabucks of investment banking partners. There are also differing requisites for entry: high grades are required for investment banking, while, with the right experience, it's still possible to be hired as a stockbroker without even a college degree.

Yet there are also common threads. Wall Street careers are demanding, and, accordingly, demand evidence of excellence as the price of admission. An undergraduate concentration in Business, Accounting, or Economics is not a requirement. In fact, the opposite is true: there are premiums for those who can think, analyze, and write. Financial firms tend to favor the liberal arts or humanities graduates who can demonstrate first these talents and second some evidence of quantitative ability.

Thus the Political Science (or English, History, Psychology, or even Art History) major who has taken some courses in Economics, Business, Accounting, Math, and/or Computer Science, is the ideal candidate for most of these positions. The Business major who has taken few Humanities courses will find it necessary to prove the ability for subjective analysis and the ability to write.

Within the last few years, the distinctions between banks, investment banks, brokerage and other financial firms have begun to blur as these institutions have evolved into financial services companies offering a broad range of services to their clients. Citicorp's competitors now include Sears and Merrill Lynch as well as Bank of America and Chase Manhattan.

In 1933, in the dismal aftermath of the ruin of banks that had sustained whopping losses from securities transactions and were wiped out along with the individual fortunes of their depositors, Congress passed the Glass-Steagall Act. The Act required that firms that accept deposits (banks) be separate from firms that underwrite corporate securities (investment banks). Thus the venerable Wall Street firm of J. P. Morgan—the House of Morgan—split off their investment banking arm while retaining their position as a commercial bank. The two resultant independent firms are today known as J. P. Morgan & Co. (holding company for the bank Morgan Guaranty Trust Company) and Morgan Stanley & Co., Inc.

Debate concerning the possible repeal of the Glass-Steagall Act continues to rage. While it is impossible to say when the battle between banks, brokers, and regulators may yield a truce with the legislated demolition of the Glass-Steagall barrier, efforts by state-chartered banks and innovative moves by financial services companies have gone so far in circumventing the Act that its eventual repeal may be almost a non-event.

In recent years, it is the mergers and consolidatons of financial firms that have revolutionized the way Wall Street does business. There have been mergers within industries, as with the Merrill Lynch acquisitions of White, Weld, in 1978 and, more recently, the absorption of A. G. Becker. Shearson/American Express enhanced their investment banking and trading capabilities with the acquisition of the old-line firm of Lehman Brothers.

Even more newsworthy has been the joining of firms in previously-separate financial industries, as with the merger of Prudential Insurance and Bache, Halsey, Stuart, a brokerage firm. The resultant firm, Prudential-Bache Securities, offers to individual clients of the brokerage firm subsidiary the recognition of the great financial strength of the insurance parent, while insurance customers of Prudential are now ready prospects for the full financial services, including stock brokerage and financial planning, offered by the brokerage firm.

Sears, in acquiring Coldwell Banker (a real estate brokerage firm) and Dean Witter Reynolds (a securities brokerage firm) and American Express, in its acquisition of Shearson Loeb Rhoades, both made financial history as they extended even further the definition of financial and consumer services. Banks such as Security Pacific National Bank of Los Angeles and San Francisco-based BankAmerica Corp. have pioneered in entering the discount brokerage business.

These extensions of the traditional definitions of the financial industries are both confusing and exciting to the person choosing a career. They're confusing because it's no longer so simple to decide that you want to be in commercial banking rather than investment banking, because there is increasing overlap between the two. Yet they're exciting because the opportunities for those who are prepared to be creative and innovative as new challenges bring new opportunities are greater than ever before.

For the job applicant, there is one additional layer of confusion, because separate units of these huge financial services firms tend to do their own hiring. Thus, one might apply separately to Prudential Insurance for a career in the investment management of their assets, and to individual Pru-Bache branch offices for a position as a stockbroker. The same is true of most financial firms: in commercial banks, there is usually a central Personnel or Human Resources office, usually with a College Relations department, that coordinates the hiring of trainees for formal training programs in commercial lending, retail banking, operations, and computer systems; but other divisions such as investment banking, trading, and trust may be responsible for their own hiring.

Even the stock brokerage firms are confusing. Within Merrill Lynch, for example, one would apply to the College Relations Department of Personnel for a position in management training such as their Corporate Internship Program, to the investment banking division (Merrill Lynch Capital Markets) for a position in corporate finance, to the research department (Merrill Lynch Research) for a position as a Research Assistant; and to individual branch offices to be hired as a stockbroker.

The dedicated job applicant interested in a position with one of these firms must first talk with someone in the organization to determine exactly which department or division should be contacted for which job (and to determine the correct name of the department). For many of the largest financial firms, this has been done for you in the Appendix to this book; for others, call to find out where your inquiries should be sent.

An understanding of certain terms is important in our discussion of financial careers. More definitions are provided in the chapters in which they are discussed. Your interviewers will expect you to understand these terms and concepts.

Institution. A financial firm that invests large amounts of money. This includes insurance companies, mutual funds, the trust departments of banks, investment counseling or investment management firms, and the pension funds of large corporations. These institutions control the vast majority of the assets traded in U.S. securities markets.

Retail. A retail client of a bank or brokerage firm is an individual or small business. For example, a Kidder, Peabody Retail Account Executive is a stockbroker who works exclusively with individual investors and their businesses. Retail banking (also called branch banking) services these same clients.

Buy Side. Institutional investors constitute the Buy Side. When they are buying and selling securities and obtaining research concerning these securities from the research analysts of brokerage firms, they are *buying* the services of the brokerage firms on the Sell Side.

Bull Market. A market in which prices are going up.

Bear Market. A market in which prices are going down.

Sell Side. Brokerage firms that offer their services and research to institutional clients constitute the Sell Side.

Equity. A common or preferred stock is an equity security, which means that it represents ownership in a company. A trader trading common or preferred stocks is an equity, or stock, trader.

Bonds/Fixed-Income Securities/Debt Securities. A bond is the agreement that results when a corporation (or goverment or municipality) borrows money from the investing public. Thus, bonds are debt securities. Because a fixed rate of interest to be paid on the debt is usually agreed upon when a bond is created (*issued*), they are also called fixed-income securities. In recent years many debt securities have been issued with interest rates that change from time to time, according to a preset formula. These *floating-rate* securities are generally handled by the same individuals who work with fixed-income securities.

The Over-the-Counter Market. A market for securities that are not listed on an exchange such as the New York Stock Exchange. OTC traders communicate via computer terminals that display what buyers and sellers are will to bid and offer. The term generally refers to stock trading, although bonds are also traded in the OTC market.

Capital Markets. Worldwide markets for securities, including stocks, bonds (including U.S Government securities) and other financial instruments.

Private Placement. A securities transaction involving a private agreement between two or more parties. It is neither offered to the general public nor executed on an exchange. Generally, these transactions are arranged by investment bankers and involve large sums of money committed by institutions. For example, a large insurance company may invest $5 million in a growing high technology company by buying that amount of convertible preferred stock directly from the company rather than on an exchange.

For further definitions and explanations of different type of securities and their markets, read Engel and Boyd's classic *How to*

Buy Stocks (see "Resources"), available in paperback and in any library. Common and preferred stock, bonds and debentures, the exchanges and the OTC markets, and many other securities terms are discussed clearly and completely.

A Word to the Women

The opportunities at the entry level on Wall Street are today no different for women than they are for men. Although there are very few women at the highest levels of financial institutions, the vast numbers of talented and qualified women in the pipeline pushing the partner (or managing director or senior vice president) level will soon mandate a change. Fewer women than men may choose to make the compromise in lifestyle necessary to fulfill the demands of these top-tier positions, but there will still be many who make the commitment and are accordingly raised to these higher levels. By the time that choice must be made for those just starting out on Wall Street today, there will be abundant opportunity at all levels for both women and men.

Chapter 6

Commercial Banking

Bankers Are Just Like Anybody Else,
Except Richer.
—Ogden Nash

Commercial Lending

ALTHOUGH COMMERCIAL BANKS are enhancing their services at a
rapid pace as they extend into new areas in the financial market-
place, such as discount brokerage and investment banking, the
primary function of most commercial banks is still that of lending, or wholesale banking.

The primary customers of a commercial bank are corporations, large and small. These corporate customers borrow money
to finance their growth, make deposits of their excess cash, buy
securities traded by the bank, utilize sophisticated trading techniques to minimize their exposure in foreign currencies, and may
take advantage of many other bank services.

Governments, both domestic and foreign, are also major
bank customers. Indeed, concern about the obligations of foreign
nations to U.S. banks is front-page news.

In commercial lending, commercial bank loan officers research the creditworthiness of corporations applying for loans
from the bank, and decide whether they are a good credit risk. In
today's competitive financial services environment, loan officers
do a lot more than just lend money. Loan officers are the key
people within the bank responsible for maintaining the relationship with each client. They work intensively with clients to determine their financing needs and sell them other bank services,
including cash management and sophisticated financial trading
activities such as currency hedging. In order to do this, the loan
officers interact extensively with other areas of the bank.

Bank lending groups are usually organized to serve one type of client. There may be separate groups serving foreign governments, foreign corporations, municipalities, and domestic corporations. These groups may be further subdivided into geographic regions or, in the case of corporations, by industry. For example, separate lending groups may serve domestic energy companies and domestic high-technology companies.

The international division services the financial needs of foreign corporations and governments and the foreign subsidiaries of U.S. multinational companies. Minimizing the risks of fluctuations in foreign currencies is an important part of administering international loans. Fluency in a foreign language and a willingness to frequently travel abroad are necessary for international bankers.

Banks compete aggressively to win business from healthy corporations. Many banks have a separate New Business Group within the commercial lending division. This group has primary responsibility for the development of business from new clients —in other words, *prospecting*. In other banks, loan officers are expected to prospect for new business as well as service their existing accounts. Even in banks that have new business groups, bankers are expected to bring in some new business. For established loan officers, new business results not so much from *cold calling* (contacting new prospective customers who have not expressed any previous interest in the bank) as from using their contacts—for example, developing loan business for the bank with a corporation that has its President on the Board of Directors of a client corporation. Bankers prospect socially, as well—fellow golfers, squash players, and club members are all potential clients for the bank.

Most commercial lenders entertain clients extensively at lunch, dinner, athletic and cultural events. Spouses may be expected to attend. Some bankers love this aspect of their job; others find it tedious and frustrating. As intensifying competition between banks and other financial institutions has made it harder to distinguish the services of one from another, bankers sometimes feel they're competing on the basis of how many Celtics tickets they can obtain, rather than on the quality of their banking services.

Servicing their corporate clients can also mean a lot of pesky paperwork as bankers track down problems with statements and deposits. For most successful loan officers, however, this is simply a necessary part of developing and extending a relationship—providing the personal service that often makes the difference in landing and keeping the client.

Most major commercial banks offer excellent, highly-structured training programs in commercial lending. Depending on the size of the bank, they may hire a few dozen or over one hundred new employees for these programs each year. Training generally ranges from six months to as long as three years. There may be completely separate programs for those with B.A.'s and those with M.B.A.'s, or the training programs may be partially merged. Increasingly, training programs in commercial banks, especially those of major money-center banks, reflect the changes in the banking industry. While training programs for commercial lenders continue to emphasize accounting and other skills required for credit analysis, today they also include discussions of capital markets activities.

Some training programs are quite competitive, intentionally washing out the bottom 10% of training classes. Other banks are more likely to try to keep all who enter their training program within the firm. If you would prefer one system over the other, be sure to find out what the bank's policy is before you interview.

One important way in which commercial bank training programs differ is that some enroll all new hires in one training program for a period of months, then later assign them to specific areas within the bank such as project finance, the trust division, or retail banking, for further training. Other banks hire candidates for placement in a specific area, such as the international division, and train them accordingly. Others use a combination of the two methods: for example, hire new employees for one general area of banking, such as lending (a "Loan Officer Development Program"), then assign them after a short period of training to a specific lending area, such as project finance, international, or the high-technology industries.

Make sure you know whether the banks you are considering use the general or specific approach to training. Many entry-level candidates prefer the more general approach, where they will have a period of months within the training program of the bank to develop an understanding of the functions of the different divisions. Others prefer to make their decision before they are hired. Make sure the bank with which you are interviewing has a training program that is compatible with your personal career goals.

Be careful to apply only for the training programs that are really what you want. For example, a bank may offer a "Management Development Training Program," which is a good general catchall title—just the sort of thing an unfocused person like you is looking for. However, it may turn out to be quite specific, and specifically not what you had in mind. It might refer only to the development of managers for operations positions. This may or may not be the banker's career you had envisioned. Make sure you understand what the training program is before you apply.

Retail Banking

A banker is one who lends money
to the already affluent.
—Anonymous

In retail, or branch, banking, the bank's clients are individuals with bank savings and checking accounts. Branch bankers handle personal loans, auto loans, home improvement loans, Individual Retirement Accounts (IRA's) and Keogh retirement accounts, and Visa and MasterCard transactions. Small businesses are also among a branch bank's clients.

Until the late 1970's and early 1980's, individual accounts were a source of healthy profits for banks, which paid 5% interest on deposits, then loaned the money out, in many cases at more than twice that rate. The advent of the money-market mutual funds has all but closed the door on that source of funds. As depositors withdrew their funds from banks and invested in the money-market funds, retail bankers were forced to offer competitive rates to individual depositors. Today, banks and the financial supermarkets compete intensely for the individual's deposits, IRA and Keogh accounts, and brokerage business.

Many banks provide separate training programs for branch bank managers. It is possible for an individual to be running a small branch within one to three years after joining a bank.

Trust

Put not your trust in money.
Put your money in trust.
—*Oliver Wendell Holmes*

The trust departments of commercial banks manage assets for other people. The amount of assets they control is staggering. In 1983, Bankers Trust was the top trust operation, managing discretionary assets of $37.6 billion!

In addition to managing the trusts of individuals, the trust departments of banks also manage money for wealthy individuals, endowments for schools and hospitals, and pension and profit-sharing funds that are the retirement funds of corporations. In seeking to manage these funds, banks compete aggressively with investment counseling firms or investment management firms such as Alliance Capital Management Corporation or Loomis, Sayles & Company.

Banks generally take a more conservative approach to investment management than do non-bank managers. The organization of a bank trust department and the functions of staff members involved in securities management are, however, virtually identical to those of other investment management firms.

An individual may die and leave his or her assets "in trust" for children or grandchildren, with the bank appointed as trustee. It is the bank's responsibility as trustee to manage the assets in accordance with the deceased's wishes, as expressed in the trust document. Usually, this includes the management of money and securities as well as real estate and other property. The Trust Officer assigned to the account will decide how the assets are to be managed. For example, acting on advice of real estate specialists within the Trust Department, the Trust Officer may decide to sell certain real estate properties and invest the money from the sale in common stock. Typically, the common stock portfolios of trusts are managed in turn by Portfolio Managers within the Trust Department, although in some banks the Trust Officer and Portfolio Manager are the same person. Each non-trust account, such as the pension fund of a corporation or a university endowment, is similarly managed by one or more

Portfolio Managers. An individual's or institution's funds may be individually managed or pooled with those of others.

The Portfolio Manager decides what stocks should be bought and sold within the portfolio. Usually, the decisions of the Portfolio Managers are guided by an Investment Committee that sets guidelines for investments. These usually include a specific "buy list" of common stocks that they believe are acceptable for their portfolios. The amount of discretion the Portfolio Manager actually has depends on the amount of flexibility provided by the Investment Committee.

In making decisions, Portfolio Managers usually rely on four main sources of information:

1) Research Analysts within the trust department. Almost all trust departments maintain a staff of Research Analysts, each of whom follows a group of companies within one or more industries. The Analysts recommend to the Investment Committee and Portfolio Managers the stocks they believe should be bought and sold. For further discussion of this function, see Chapter 9, "Securities Research Analysis."

2) Research Analysts at brokerage firms. Each bank utilizes research reports from literally dozens of brokerage firms to augment their own research.

3) Institutional research firms (*boutiques*). These are firms whose only service is researching securities and selling their research to institutional investors.

4) The Portfolio Manager's own research and experience. Several years' experience in securities research or portfolio management is generally necessary in order to become a Portfolio Manager. These individuals rely heavily on their own experience and judgment in making buy and sell decisions. In many cases, they have been trained as Research Analysts before becoming Portfolio Managers, and are experienced in employing analytical tools for stock selection and timing.

At one time, bank trust departments were among the sleepiest niches on Wall Street. Because wealthy individuals could avoid the payment of enormous sums of money in inheritance taxes by establishing trusts, it was a virtual necessity that they do so. Intending that the trust would function for their children and grandchildren, it was essential that an enduring institution such as a bank be appointed as trustee in order to ensure that the trustee would be able to assume the responsibilities at the time trusteeship was required. Thus the trust money was handed to the banks on a silver platter. It was a gentleman's business, and a non-competitive one.

With the entry of the banks' portfolio management services into the arena of corporate retirement plans in recent years, however, the activity of bank trust departments has changed greatly. It is now strongly competitive—an environment in which performance rather than relationships determines who gets the business. Those money managers who achieve the best increases in value of assets under their management are those who retain their clients and receive new clients from the competition.

Banks differ as to whether they hire B.A.'s or only M.B.A.'s into their trust departments. More and more, an M.B.A. is required for entry-level positions as Research Analysts or Assistants. Often B.A.'s are hired for positions with titles such as "Administrative Assistant" or "Portfolio Assistant," which can be more promising than they sound, as positions in which Trust Officers and Portfolio Managers are groomed.

Increasingly, bank trust departments are requiring Research Analysts and Portfolio Managers to participate in the Charter Financial Analyst (C.F.A.) program. See Chapter 9, "Securities Research Analysis" for a discussion of this program.

Investment Banking in Commercial Banks

Commercial banks also engage in some investment banking activities. Because the Glass-Steagall Act prohibits them from underwriting corporate securities, commercial banks underwrite exclusively non-corporate securities such as municipal bonds, which are issued by a governmental or quasi-governmental body such as a state or city government, hospital, college or university, housing authority, turnpike, or port authority. Banks also offer their advice on financial transactions, including mergers and acquisitions, to corporations and governments for a fee. They may also arrange private placements of stocks and bonds. Many major banks are today participating in the venture capital markets.

In all of these areas, banks compete directly with investment banking and brokerage houses offering the same services.

Commercial banks typically fill positions in their investment banking departments with individuals who have had substantial experience in other areas of the bank, or by hiring investment bankers from an investment banking firm. Entry-level positions in this area are few, and are generally limited to M.B.A.'s.

Regardless of whether the Glass-Steagall Act is repealed, allowing banks to underwrite corporate securities, banks can be expected to continue to move aggressively in the area of investment banking. This will expand the career paths open to bankers, especially those able to contribute creative thinking and innovative marketing skills. It should also continue to cause bankers' salaries to rise to levels more comparable with those of investment bankers, a trend that has already begun.

Trading

*Business is a combination
of war and sport.
—Emile Herzog*

Many commercial banks maintain substantial trading operations, primarily in government, municipal, and money-market securities, and in foreign currencies. Customers of these trading desks are corporations and institutions, regardless of whether they are also clients of the bank's lending division. A bank may only trade securities such as municipal bonds, or may also arrange sophisticated transactions such as currency swaps and interest-rate hedges.

There are limited opportunities for big-time trading outside of New York City. Most investment banks' trading operations are headquartered there, and the largest bank trading operations are those of the New York City money-center banks. Major commercial banks outside of New York offer newcomers an opportunity to learn the profession, but real advancement usually requires a move to New York.

Because investment bank trading desks dominate most markets, a full discussion of the trading function is given in "Sales and Trading" in Chapter 7, "Investment Banking."

Treasury

Like any corporation, the bank must manage its monetary assets and liabilities: invest its excess cash to earn interest, and borrow or raise equity capital to fulfill its cash needs and meet regulatory requirements. It must minimize carrying costs, or interest, on what it borrows. The Treasury Department of a bank manages this function.

Operations and Systems

Commercial banks have monumental requirements for operations processing in all aspects of their business. Maintaining customers' deposit and loan accounts, handling deposits and withdrawals, including Automated Teller Machine (ATM) processing, and check processing are only part of their operational activities. Accordingly, their data processing requirements are immense. Banks often offer separate training programs for B.A.'s in Operations Management and Computer Systems. For Operations Management, they are looking for potential managers, so communication skills are especially important. In Computer Systems, a technical background in mathematics or the sciences is favored, with prior computer experience a plus. For both, a knowledge of accounting and finance is helpful.

Other Bank Services

Commercial banks are extending their financial services into new areas virtually every day. Hundreds have entered the discount brokerage business, in which the discount brokerage firm executes securities transactions such as the purchase and sale of stocks and bonds for customers but provides no advice. Unlike full-service brokerage firms that employ highly-paid salespeople to advise their customers on what actions to take, discount brokers pass the savings from not paying a sales force along to the customer in the form of lower commission charges on transactions. Most banks entering this business, like BankAmerica Corp., parent of Bank of America, do so by acquiring a discount broker. Others are entering into joint ventures with discount firms.

Banks are also selling their operational capability to other financial institutions. Columbus, Ohio's BankOne Corporation

experienced meteoric growth by providing the banking operations for Merrill Lynch's revolutionary Cash Management Account. Other banks, such as State Street Bank & Trust Company
of Boston, handle processing for many of the nation's mutual
funds. Most major commercial banks provide stock transfer services to corporations.

What Do Bankers Earn?

*Financial success is never having
to balance your checkbook.*
—*Benjamin Graham*

Even within the last few years, there have been dramatic
changes in bankers' compensation, as banks have competed for
talented people with other Wall Street firms. Entry-level salaries
for B.A.'s are $15,000 to $25,000, depending primarily on geographic location. M.B.A.'s start at $25,000 to $40,000, depending
on the candidate's qualifications and the location of the bank. In
New York City, starting salaries are comparable to those of investment banks, although, in general, bankers' total compensation is less than that of investment bankers, as commercial
banks rarely offer the big bonuses that are common at investment
banks in good years.

In a New York City bank, Vice Presidents may make $50,000
to $150,000 in total compensation. Outside of New York, the
range tends to be closer to $30,000 to $100,000. Although, as we
have noted, the pace of work at commercial banks is speeding
up, it is still unusual for commercial bankers to work more than
a fifty-to-sixty-hour average week. For investment bankers, on
the other hand, it is unusual to work less than fifty or sixty hours
a week.

Why Become a Commercial Banker?

Commercial bank training programs offer outstanding opportunities for entry-level candidates, with or without an M.B.A.
degree. For someone who desires a highly-structured environment, the training is excellent. It allows exceptional flexibility in
choosing future career paths, either within banking or in another
industry. Many corporate Controllers, Treasurers, and Chief Financial Officers began their careers as bank lending officers.

Commercial banking is appropriate for the individual who prefers a more bureaucratic, seniority-conscious environment to the entrepreneurial, performance-based atmosphere of investment banking, securities brokerage, or securities research.

Most major banks offer full tuition reimbursement plans that allow you to take evening courses leading to an M.B.A. or, in some cases, a law degree at local colleges and universities. If you can find time in your life to do it, this is an outstanding benefit for those who don't want to halt their career while they enroll in a full-time two-or-three-year course. In most cases, with a full schedule of two courses per semester, including summers, you may earn an M.B.A. degree in three years.

Not least among the reasons to join a commercial bank is the wide network of contacts that arise as classmates from training programs spread out through corporate America as they leave the bank.

The increasingly-competitive environment in financial services offers new opportunities to the newest crop of commercial bankers, as the ability to provide creative management and innovative thinking becomes vital to the once-stodgy banks as they continue to expand into the previously-uncharted waters of capital markets and financial services.

Why Not Become a Commercial Banker?

Some commercial bank training program trainees are dismayed to find themselves back in school again. Some programs require a full year of classroom study, which can be frustrating for someone eager to launch a career. Others don't like the training programs because they're too competitive.

Although it is primarily the dynamic world of the major money-center banks that is described in this book, many banks are still in the backwater. There are banks where "banker's hours" prevail, and where young up-and-comers may find their career path blocked by a somnolent Old Guard. One (but only one) of the 200 top banks named in the Appendix to this book still has banking hours from 9:00 AM to 3:00 PM.

Other than these, the only other major reason not to be a banker is because there is something else that you'd rather do. Perhaps you are driven to aim for an investment banker's dazzling salary. Or you may prefer a more entrepreneurial environment than that offered by most banks. Perhaps you would rather devote your career to researching stocks and bonds, or feel that you would have more freedom and earnings potential as a securities salesperson than as a commercial lender.

What Kind of Person Are They Looking For?

Commercial banks want bright, well-rounded people who have both quantitative ability and the ability to write and communicate well. Grades are important, though not as critical as for investment banks. Banks hire candidates with every major: English and Political Science as well as Economics and Mathematics. Because the bank training programs are so comprehensive, they tend to require only evidence that you are comfortable with numbers rather than a large number of Business, Accounting, or Economics courses. Because interaction with others, both clients and colleagues within the bank, is vital, banks look for evidence of leadership or teamwork, such as participation in college government or team sports.

Fluency in foreign languages is a big plus for international departments. Applicants should learn which banks have extensive operations in countries in which their languages are spoken. For example, a Spanish major is an excellent candidate for the Bank of Boston, which has large Central and South American activities.

How to Apply

Use your network to contact people in the areas of the bank in which you are interested. At the same time, if you are applying for any of the training programs, send a letter and resume to Personnel. Find out which departments, such as Trading, Trust, or International, do not fill positions from the pool of individuals in the training programs, and contact them directly.

Suggested Reading

"Bankers as Brokers," *Business Week,* April 11, 1983.

"Banking's Squeeze," *Business Week,* April 12, 1982.

Linda Sandler, "Investment Banking Proves a Tough Field for Commercial Banks," *The Wall Street Journal,* September 19, 1984.

Chapter 7

Investment Banking

Finance is the art of passing money
from one hand to another
until it finally disappears.
—Leonard L. Levinson

FIGURE 12 LISTS the top investment banking firms. About half are privately-owned: Goldman, Sachs, for example, is still a partnership; others, such as Kidder Peabody, are corporations. Seven are publicly-held corporations whose stock, or their parent company's stock, is traded on an exchange. In a partnershiip, the highest rank is usually that of Managing Partner; in a corporation, Managing Director.

Investment banking firms or investment banking divisions within larger financial services firms are usually divided into several major areas: corporate finance, public finance, sales and trading, securities research, and other areas such as venture capital or money management.

The Corporate and Public Finance Functions

The primary role of an investment bank is to assist its clients—corporations and governments—in building financial value by raising capital, through merger and acquisition, and via other strategies. They underwrite and distribute securities through both public and private financings, both in the United States and abroad.

Corporate finance staff members may be generalists or specialists. Generalists are usually organized by industry group, such as energy, financial services, utilities, or high technology. Specialty departments include merger and acquisition, private

Figure 12

Investment Banking Firms

Special-Bracket and Major-Bracket Firms	*Firms Privately or Publicly Owned*
Alex. Brown & Sons Inc. (Baltimore)	Public
Bear Stearns & Co. Inc.	Public
Dean Witter Reynolds, Inc.	Public (Sears)
Dillon, Read & Co. Inc	Private
Donaldson, Lufkin & Jenrette Securities Corporation	Private (Equitable Life)
Drexel Burnham Lambert Inc.	Private
The First Boston Corporation	Public
Goldman, Sachs & Co.	Private
Hambrecht & Quist, Inc. (San Francisco)	Private
E. F. Hutton & Co., Inc.	Public
Kidder, Peabody & Co., Inc.	Private
Lazard Freres & Co. (NYC, London, Paris)	Private
Merrill Lynch Capital Markets	Public (Merrill Lynch & Co.)
Morgan Stanley & Co., Inc.	Public
Paine Webber Inc.	Public
Prudential-Bache Securities	Private
L.F. Rothschild, Unterberg, Towbin Inc.	Public
Salomon Brothers, Inc.	Public (Phibro-Salomon)
Shearson Lehman Brothers Inc.	Public (American Express)
Smith Barney, Harris Upham & Co. Inc.	Private
Wertheim & Co. Inc.	Private

placement, real estate, tax shelter, and leasing. These departments may assist corporations that are clients of the corporate finance group, or may initiate their own transactions. Today, major investment banks have specialists in literally dozens of different financing products and services.

Public finance groups work with governments and municipalities, and may be subdivided according to the type of governmental body or geographically. In the discussion that follows, the role of investment bankers in working with corporate clients is discussed; when the client is a government seeking to borrow money, the process is similar for public as for corporate finance.

As a corporation grows, its management may find that they need more money than they can easily obtain themselves. They can borrow the money they need from banks, but banks typically want to be paid back within a relatively short period of time, such as one to seven years. They will usually charge a rate of interest that varies with the prevailing prime rate.

The company may want more permanent capital: either money obtained from issuing (selling) common stock, which is money that never has to be repaid, but that gives the purchaser a percentage of ownership in the company; or money obtained by issuing bonds, which is borrowed and must be repaid, but not for a period of several or many years and which usually carries a fixed rate of interest.

In order to issue either common stock or bonds, the corporation will usually hire an investment bank, a firm that specializes in finding investors to invest in or finance corporations and governments that need money. The investors may be individuals buying a few hundred shares of stock, or large financial institutions lending millions of dollars to the company.

Investment bankers analyze the needs of their clients and make recommendations to them on the best way to obtain the money they need. For example, a young computer company may question whether they should *go public* (issue stock to the public for the first time). An investment bank will help them decide whether to do this, or whether they would be better off by postponing a public offering and raising the money privately now. In this case, the investment banking firm will solicit the interest of a few large institutions or corporations to invest in the company—a *private placement*.

A large New York Stock Exchange-listed health care company may need a new manufacturing facility. Their investment bankers will help them determine how to finance the plant—whether to lease or mortgage it, issue more stock, or issue bonds and borrow the money.

Once the type of offering has been decided upon, the investment banking firm initiates the offering by managing the preparation of legal documents required to meet government regulations regarding securities offerings. When governmental approval has been obtained and market conditions are right, they will underwrite the issue and sell, or distribute, the stock or bonds to the public.

Part of the process of issuing securities to the public involves complying with extensive government disclosure regulations under the watchful eye of the Securities and Exchange Commission (SEC). For this purpose, a *registration statement* including a *prospectus* is prepared for each offering. The registration statement is for the SEC; a copy of the prospectus is given to every potential investor in the offering. These lengthy documents contain extensive information on the finances, business, and management of the company. All material facts about the company and the offering must be disclosed. Even small errors can have enormous legal and financial ramifications; thus, their careful preparation is vital.

Under the direction of senior members of the team, much of the gathering and compilation of information and figures and checking for accuracy is done by the Analysts and Associates of the investment banking firm. They work closely with company counsel, their accountants, and counsel for the underwriters. They really do spend entire nights at the printer's, waiting for proofs and checking the accuracy of every word and number.

Where necessary, as for companies that have never before issued stock to the public, or for certain unlisted securities, the investment bankers also obtain permission from each of the state governments to sell the issue in their state. Once a security has been approved by a state, it is said to be *blue-skyed* in that state.

While awaiting SEC approval, which can take from one to six weeks, the *managing*, or *lead* investment banking firm forms a *syndicate, or underwriting group,* of other investment bankers. Each of these firms commits to underwrite a certain amount of the securities. That means that, once the price of the securities is agreed upon, the underwriters guarantee payment of that amount to the corporation issuing the securities. The underwriters then attempt to sell the securities to the public.

Although they have gathered non-binding *indications of interest* in the securities from clients prior to the offering, it is still possible that the underwriters will be unable to sell all of the securities. Thus, the investment bankers have taken on, *or underwritten*, all of the risk of the offering from the company issuing the securities. The "fee" the underwriters earn for their services is the difference between the price they pay for the securities and the price at which they sell them (the *discount*). They bear the risk of loss depending on what happens to the price of the securities in the few days after an offering (the *aftermarket*). Many millions of dollars have been lost on a single deal by a single underwriter. Thus an investment banker's skill at evaluating the securities markets and determining at which price securities should come to market is vital.

The investment bank managing the offering will also form a *selling group* of other investment banks and brokerage firms that agree to help sell the securities. Unlike underwriters, selling group members do not guarantee payment for the securities to the corporation.

Each investment banking firm involved in the offering then offers the securities to the institutional and retail clients of the firm through their sales force of Account Executives (brokers). The number of brokers in investment banking firms varies widely—from major-bracket firms with fewer than one hundred, to Merrill Lynch, with more than ten thousand.

As part of the firm's efforts to sell the securities, the investment bankers usually join with the Institutional Account Executives to take the company's management on a "road show": a whirlwind tour of major cities in the United States and, often, Europe. In each city, they give presentations on the company and the offering to major institutional investors.

When the Securities and Exchange Commission has cleared the offering, the investment bankers bring it to the market. They do so by first discussing with the issuer market conditions prevailing at that time: for bonds, current levels and trends of interest rates; for stocks, what is happening in the stock market as a

whole, in their industry group, and, for stocks that are already
traded, with their own stock. For bonds, the investment bankers
and the company's management negotiate the interest rate they
will have to pay: the banker wants a rate high enough to attract
investor interest, yet naturally the company wants to pay the
lowest possible interest rate.

For an initial offering of common stock in a company going
public for the first time, the investment bankers and the management of the company try to determine the best possible price at
which to offer the stock to the public. If it is priced too high, no
one will buy it; if too low, the stock will soar right after the offering and the company will be miffed because they didn't get as
much money from the public as they might have. For a stock that
is already traded in the public markets, the new common stock to
be offered is usually priced at or very close to the closing price of
the stock on the day of the offering.

Investment banks also provide their clients with advice on
financial strategy, capital structure, and mergers and acquisitions ("M & A"). Corporations interested in acquiring another
firm, selling their own firm, divesting themselves of an un-
profitable division by selling it to another company, or trying to
avoid an unwanted takeover by another firm, pay substantial
fees to investment bankers for their advice and assistance.

> *Where the willingness is great,*
> *the difficulties cannot be great.*
> —*Machiavelli*

Prior to any of this happening, however, the investment
bankers must demonstrate what is increasingly becoming the
most important skill of all: getting the business. Even a decade
ago, investment banking was relatively non-competitive. Once a
company like Exxon had established a relationship with an investment banking firm, it was unthinkable that they would shift
their allegiance to another banker.

Today, however, competition is cutthroat, and investment
bankers must continue to convince their clients that they can
outperform the others in many ways:

1) their experience in similar transactions;
2) their understanding of the client's business;

3) the degree to which they can fulfill the client's wishes for distribution of the securities (for example, a company may want 80% of issued shares placed with institutional investors and only 20% with individuals, or vice versa);

4) the speed with which they can respond to the client's need to raise capital;

5) the readiness with which they can sell the deal—if it becomes known that an offering is not selling well, it reflects poorly on both the corporation and the investment banker; the largest investment banking and brokerage firms can offer massive sales support in placing securities for offerings;

6) on the firm's trading capabilities and ability to maintain a good market for the securities;

7) on the research coverage they will provide on the company;

8) on their creativity in offering new financing techniques or their ability to address new markets;

9) on their effectiveness in judging market conditions and thus making pricing and timing decisions.

The investment bankers will call into play their experience and expertise in presenting their firm's excellence in these areas. In addition to these objective reasons, however, the personal chemistry between the investment bankers and the management of the client company will be an important factor in the client's selection of an investment banking firm.

Until a few years ago, the prestigious firm of Morgan Stanley consistently refused to co-manage a deal with any other firm; today, recognizing the competitive environment, they routinely do so. A corporation with hybrid goals might find no one firm with sufficient resources to handle the deal. For example, a growing computer firm might recognize the high-technology expertise of Hambrecht & Quist or Robertson, Colman & Stephens, but would want them to co-manage with a larger firm such as Merrill Lynch.

The advent of Rule 415 (*shelf registration* — see "Suggested Reading" at the end of this chapter) brought additional competitive pressures to investment banks. Now certain larger issuers could file with the SEC up to two years in advance of an actual offering. They could then move quickly to sell the securities "off the shelf" when market conditions were advantageous, using any investment banking firm. Rule 415 spelled the end of that era on Wall Street where relationships were paramount; today size and capital, sales and trading capabilities, and the resultant ability to move on a moment's notice, are all-important.

Many firms, large and small, have been influenced by these competitive pressures, as well as the inherent volatility of the securities markets, to merge and consolidate, such as, recently, A.G. Becker with Merrill Lynch, and Lehman Brothers and Shearson Loeb Rhoades with American Express.

Investment bankers typically work sixty to eighty hours a week, and there are many weeks they work over one hundred hours!

Entry-level positions for B.A.'s at most of the special-bracket and major-bracket firms are the same: a two-year position as a Financial Analyst, after which they are expected to go to business or law school or find another job. It is unusual for an investment bank to allow a Financial Analyst to stay beyond the two-year period, although it is sometimes possible to arrange a transfer to a branch office or to another division of the firm such as trading or institutional or retail brokerage sales.

Although it is no longer true that an Analyst position at a top investment bank guarantees admission to the top business schools, it can be an important advantage.

Once armed with an M.B.A. degree, you may be hired as an Associate, generally working from three to five years before becoming a Vice President. Achievement of the top level within the firm—that of Managing Partner or Managing Director—generally takes ten years or more.

Training varies from firm to firm. Some offer an initial one or two months of classroom study, others merely a series of lectures. In all, most of the training is on the job and over your head, combining tremendous responsibility from day one with one of the steepest learning curves on Wall Street. It's not a highly-structured training environment like that of a commercial bank. Also unlike a commercial bank, you can forget about getting an M.B.A. in the evening—you'll be working.

Most financing projects are worked on by a team consisting of three to five people: one or more Analysts, one or more Associates, a Vice President, and a Managing Director. Analysts and Associates generally work on several teams simultaneously, and must learn to balance the resultant conflicting demands. They are primarily responsible for gathering and analyzing financial information to be used in connection with offerings or other transactions, such as collecting data for financial comparisons with similar companies and securities. Preparation of data used in registration statements and prospectuses also largely falls to Analysts and Associates. They combine information from the firm's library and computer data bases and their Research Analysts with data provided by the client to present the company's current and historical financial status together with information about their business, products, markets, competition, management and directors. There is extensive opportunity for Analysts and Associates to interact with both colleagues and clients.

Sales and Trading

> There are only two emotions in Wall Street:
> fear and greed.
> —William M. LeFevre

Trading is a vital function of investment banks. Equity trading desks of major investment banks may buy and sell hundreds of thousands of shares a day. Traders in U.S. Government securities move many millions of dollars' worth of Treasury bills, notes, and bonds every day.

The Sales and Trading Division of many investment banks has salespeople, responsible for the relationship with institutional clients, acting as liaison with the traders. The salespeople develop and maintain the relationship by offering ideas that benefit the clients. A successful salesperson must have a thorough knowledge of the securities markets and the sophisticated financial strategies employed by institutional investors, as well as the ability to sell.

Once an idea is accepted by the client, the traders execute the transaction. In other firms, the same individuals perform both the sales and trading functions.

Traders, whether employed by a commercial bank, brokerage firm or investment bank, operate in one of two ways:

1) *as a principal.* These traders have the authority to commit their firm's funds to the purchase of substantial amounts of securities, in the hope of reselling them later at a profit. Traders may own a security for minutes, hours, days, or much longer, depending upon their judgment of the direction of the market. Normally they want to keep the *inventory* of securities they have purchased at a minimum by selling them as soon as possible— the longer the securities are held, the greater the risk that they will decline in price. The principal trader's function is similar whether trading government securities (such as Treasury notes), over-the-counter stocks, municipal bonds, or other securities.

Making a market in a security is a form of principal trading. By serving as a focal point for trading in a security such as an over-the-counter stock, market makers provide a service to the company issuing the stock. Generally, the price of securities for which there is a strong, liquid market is higher than the price of those for which it is difficult to find buyers and sellers. Thus, issuers want a ready, or liquid, market for their securities. Market makers not only match buyers and sellers, but agree to buy or sell the stock into or from their own account if there are no other takers. They maintain a liquid market by trying to accommodate all orders with a minimal change in the price of the stock.

Traders expect to realize large profits and losses every day, but to earn more profits than losses over a period of time. As you would expect, if losses instead consistently exceed profits, they will be looking elsewhere for employment.

As a result, the life of a trader is hectic, fast-paced, and stressful. More ulcers, high blood pressure, and practical jokes are found on trading floors than anywhere else on Wall Street! Yet the potential for enormous earnings is there: in committing millions of dollars of their firm's capital, they can earn substantial sums for their companies, and are compensated accordingly. Most good, seasoned traders on Wall Street earn well in excess of $100,000. Some earn well over $500,000.

2) *as an agent.* Traders who act as agents merely match buy-

ers and sellers of securities. For example, one of the bank's corporate clients may wish to invest some cash for 30 days. The bank's money-market trading desk would review all suitable securities offered by other banks and brokerage firms, and would offer them to the client. In this case, the bank would earn the equivalent of a commission for its services. These traders may be simply order-takers, or they may be active salespeople selling securities that their firm has in inventory. They may be on a straight salary (often plus bonus for good performance) or commission, depending on the firm. In general, they earn far less than the principal traders or market-makers because they take less risk and generate less profit for their firm.

Often, the sales and trading departments or divisions of an investment bank do their own hiring. Entry-level positions are available at many firms that like to train new traders their way, as well as hire experienced traders.

Qualities of a successful trader include drive, an entrepreneurial spirit, and nerves of steel.

What Do Investment Bankers Earn?

*Young people, nowadays, imagine that money is everything,
and when they grow older, they know it.*
—*Oscar Wilde*

Most investment bankers are paid with a combination of salary and bonus. Starting salaries for Analysts are in the $20,000 to $30,000 range; for Associates, $35,000 to $50,000, depending on experience. In good years, both might earn bonuses of 20% to 100% of their salaries. Associates with two to three years' experience have earned over $100,000; Vice Presidents $150,000 to $300,000.

In privately-held firms such as Goldman, Sachs, Managing Partners are assumed to earn more than one million dollars a year. Although compensation for Managing Directors in the publicly-held investment banking firms is substantially less, it still is in the mid-to-high six-figure range.

Why Become an Investment Banker?

*The happiest time in any man's life is when
he is in red-hot pursuit of a dollar with a
reasonable prospect of overtaking it.*
—Josh Billings

The number one reason attracting most investment bankers to the profession is money. The lure of a six-figure income within a few short years brings hundreds of the brightest and best to Wall Street each year.

Investment banking provides an outstanding launching pad for other careers as well, such as top corporate management. When a corporation finds itself in need of a Chief Executive or Chief Financial Officer, they are almost certain to consider their investment banker.

As in commercial banking, the profession affords outstanding lifetime contacts as peers eventually move on to other firms and careers.

When these talented and hard-driving individuals pause from an eighty-hour work week to tell you why they are investment bankers, they invariably emphasize one reason: "It's fun." Fun to be constantly challenged, to do your best and to be the best; to work in a fast-paced, high-risk, intellectually-stimulating environment; to join with the top management of some of the country's biggest and best corporations in making an impact on the securities markets and the nation's economy, and fun to be paid a lot of money for doing it.

Why Not Become an Investment Banker?

The things that make investment banking one of the most exhilarating and challenging occupations in the world can make it torture for some individuals. The hours are brutal, and practically nothing short of hospitalization can spare you from them. At some firms, the atmosphere is one of friendly challege to the young Analysts and Associates; at others, more like punishment. For most, the challenge comes as much from peers as from older members of the team, as all struggle to achieve recognition and set themselves above the rest of the crowd.

Nor is there much light at the end of the tunnel. Throughout your career as an investment banker, you will be plagued with unused symphony tickets, dates left stranded, family seldom seen during the week, and cancelled vacations.

Achievement of upward mobility in an investment banking firm requires a degree of self-promotion that some may disdain. As with law, the odds against achieving promotion to Managing Partner or Managing Director may be discouraging.

Investment banking is not for those who lack discipline or extraordinary commitment to their career goal.

Where Can You Be an Investment Banker?

New York, New York. Although there are several smaller major-bracket firms with regional headquarters, such as Hambrecht & Quist in San Francisco and Alex. Brown in Baltimore, the best opportunities and exposure are in New York City.

What Kind of Person Are They Looking For?

Investment banks, more than any other type of financial firm, look for the best academic credentials. Excellent grades are a requirement. They usually must be accompanied by other evidence of leadership, such as accomplishment in sports (preferably team sports), campus government, or a team activity such as the college newspaper. Most investment banks will want to know your GMAT scores.

Majors in Business, Economics, and Accounting are not automatically favored. On the contrary, those who have a strong academic background in History, English, or Political Science, for example, are valued because they have demonstrated their ability to think, analyze, and write. Liberal Arts graduates should, however, have strong evidence of quantitative skills, with good grades in courses in Economics, Business, Accounting, or Mathematics. In some cases, a college-level course in Accounting is a prerequisite for being hired. In all cases, it is highly desirable. Familiarity with computers is becoming increasingly important.

Investment banks also look favorably on any other evidence of initiative or entrepreneurship (such as outside jobs or other money-making activities). Don't hesitate to put this information into the cover letter for your resume. If you didn't play team sports because you were working two jobs during the school year to pay your own tuition, be sure you let them know.

Investment bankers must not only have excellent financial analytical skills, but be able to present ideas and strategies articulately and convincingly both in writing and in person. Their extensive contact with individuals at the highest levels of management in client corporations also demands strong interpersonal skills; they must be likeable, interesting people.

In choosing a firm, try to develop a feeling for the way in which they work together as a team. Your interviews will give you clues. A high-pressure interview may indicate a hard-driving, pressure-cooker atmosphere.

Some firms rotate Analysts' assignments every six months to assure them exposure to all major areas (such as project finance, corporate finance, or mergers and acquisitions). Some rotate every year, or not at all. There may even be an opportunity to spend your second year in a branch office. Some companies offer formal training that may be preferable for those without a strong financial background, while others provide only on-the-job training.

How to Apply

As always, send your cover letter and resume first to your contacts within the company. Generally, an Associate or other investment banker is appointed head of recruiting each year. Where the name of the individual in charge of recruiting for 1985 graduates was available, it has been included in the Appendix to this book. In other cases, the Personnel Department of the firm will be able to give you the name of the firm's recruiter.

In many firms, you should apply separately for a position in Sales and Trading. Inquire to see whether this is the case in the firms in which you are interested.

Always follow up with phone calls. This is an entrepreneurial, telephone business. Don't hesitate to demonstrate the same kind of follow-through they will expect you to utilize with their clients and prospective clients!

Suggested Reading

A. F. Ehrbar, "Upheaval in Investment Banking," *Fortune*, August 23, 1982. Discusses Rule 415 - shelf registration.

I. Ross, "How Goldman Sachs Grew and Grew," *Fortune*, July 9, 1984.

"The Traders Take Charge—once genteel, investment banking is now rougher—and more lucrative," *Business Week*, February 20, 1984.

Chapter 8

Securities Brokerage

SECURITIES BROKERAGE FIRMS serve two primary functions: first, their investment banking activities help to raise capital for corporations and governments by placing securities with institutional and individual investors. Second, they serve as brokers to match buyers and sellers of securities.

Technically, the term "stockbroker" refers to one who has a seat on an exchange. For example, Paine Webber is a stockbroker. In common usage, however, the term refers to the salespeople who work for *full-service brokerage firms*. They are also referred to as Account Executives ("A/E's") (or, in the usage of a previous generation, as "Customer's Men"). Some firms today even call them Financial Consultants. Their official title is Registered Representative, which indicates that they have taken the New York Stock Exchange securities exam that licenses them to sell securities. Brokers in these firms offer advice to their clients as well as executing their securities transactions, unlike the *discount* brokers, who offer execution only, giving no advice to their customers.

Account Executives may be either retail or institutional brokers. The clients of a retail A/E are individuals and small businesses. Institutional A/E's serve institutional clients such as mutual funds and bank trust departments.

The Retail Account Executive

A salesman is an optimist
who finds the world full of promising potential.
—*Jerry Dashkin*

Today, most of the major brokerage firms are also "financial supermarkets," offering a broad range of products and services to their retail, or individual, clients. In 1975, Merrill Lynch proudly boasted that they offered their clients "29 different ways to invest." Today, the same firm offers over one hundred different types of investments.

Today's stockbrokers can sell their customers common and preferred stock; mutual funds; government, corporate, and municipal bonds; stock options; gold and silver; tax shelters in real estate, oil and gas drilling, movies, equipment leasing and other areas; venture capital opportunities; sophisticated "central asset" cash management money-market accounts; home mortgage financing; loans using their securities or even their home as collateral; life insurance products, including annuities; professional portfolio management and financial planning for a fee; even subscriptions to financial publications.

As a result of their ability to offer such diverse products and services, stockbrokers' fortunes are no longer dictated by the ups and downs of the stock market or the vagaries of the interest rate cycle. At the same time, the broker's life has become much more complex. The increased number of investment vehicles increases the number of clients brokers can serve and the number and size of transactions their clients will undertake, but requires more time spent studying and preparing sales presentations.

In order to be licensed as a Registered Representative, the broker must pass the difficult six-hour General Securities Registered Representative's (Series 7) Examination. Training for the exam ranges from the one-week crash courses employed by many small firms to the comprehensive four-month training programs offered by the largest brokerage houses. In addition, most brokers today are licensed to trade listed stock options and to sell life insurance products.

Most stockbrokers are paid by commission. In the large firms, beginning brokers are paid a salary that may dwindle on a preset time schedule. Some firms expect the broker to be paid a salary for only one year; sometimes as much as two; rarely more. Generally, the broker is also paid a share of commissions when they exceed the salary.

A broker receives as income a *payout* of roughly 30% to 50% of the commissions the customer pays to the firm. For example, if, in a given year, a broker's customers paid an aggregate of $100,000 in commissions on transactions, the broker would earn between $30,000 and $50,000.

Despite the fancy names some firms give stockbrokers, a broker is a salesperson. An Account Executive must remain chained to the telephone for at least the first two years, prospecting for new customers. Brokerage firms do not hand over a client list to beginning brokers. A few inactive accounts and leads from newspaper and magazine ads offering the firm's services are all that the rookie can count on. A new broker is expected to build a client base alone and with minimal direct assistance.

The large firms offer excellent training in the products and services of the firm. They may also, both during the training period and on an ongoing basis, offer training in sales techniques, but it is up to the broker to go out and sell.

The new broker's day is spent on the telephone, trying to reach new prospective clients, mostly businesspeople, who do not want to take the call because they already have a broker. Successful brokers not only get past the secretary or call screener, but, in a very few seconds, convince the prospect that they have some ideas that are worth listening to. Approaches vary: some highly successful brokers merely try to get prospects to talk, or to "qualify" them: do they have money to invest or not? Others give a sales idea right away: "Our firm has targeted three stocks that we believe could show immediate appreciation. Are you interested?" Others try and arrange an appointment with the prospect.

A new broker's evenings are spent visiting prospects or on the telephone, contacting prospects at home. Some people are eating dinner, others are watching *Dynasty*, and some are asleep, but a few may actually be willing to talk to a broker.

Whom does a broker call on as prospects? Fortunately, names are easy to come by. There are lists of high-net-worth or high-income individuals (business owners, Mercedes buyers, subscribers to *Inc.* magazine). Some brokers use the white pages or Yellow Pages; others enjoy knocking on doors of small businesses and meeting people directly.

A new broker is not an investment executive, nor a financial consultant, nor a technical stock market analyst. A new broker does not sit in a handsome office with computer on desk, reading in-depth research reports about the stock market or the high-technology industry while waiting for clients to call.

When I started as a rookie with Merrill Lynch in 1975, there was a fellow whose desk was in the same row of desks as mine. It was necessary for him to pass my desk on the way to the men's room. Every time he did, if he saw that I was reading something—no matter what it was—he grabbed it from my hand, threw it in the trash, and went on his way without a word. His message was clear: get on the phone and do your reading at night! That fellow was the legendary Dick Greene, who today is the Number One producer in Merrill Lynch. In 1984, Dick grossed more than four million dollars, earning for himself a princely income in excess of one and a half million dollars.

A successful stockbroker must possess extraordinary drive. "Self-starting" is not strong enough to express the motivation needed to keep trying, call after call, rejection after rejection, to find a receptive prospect. Once a broker acquires a "book" of clients, it's possible to spend large amounts of time handling paperwork and administrative details—activities that detract from more productive uses of time.

As a broker becomes established and more productive, the firm provides more support to deal with these details. An established broker leaves them to a Sales Assistant. But it's not unusual for new brokers to be assigned one Sales Assistant for five or six brokers, which is more than even the most competent S.A. can handle. As a result, 25% of a new broker's time can be consumed with paperwork. Failure to take care of client questions and complaints, however, invariably leads to the loss of the client and more prospecting to replace the ones who are lost.

Experienced, successful brokers have some relief from the relentless pressures of prospecting. Those who do a good job for their clients, keeping them happy and making them money, will have a steady stream of new accounts from referrals from satisfied customers. Working with an established client base, a broker spends more time researching investment ideas and discussing them with clients and less time prospecting.

> *Good counselors lack no clients.*
> —*William Shakespeare*

Contrary to popular belief, even experienced brokers work far longer than market hours (10:00 A.M. to 4:00 P.M.). Most successful brokers hit their desk no later than 8:30 A.M.—time to read *The Wall Street Journal*, attend a morning research meeting, and have problems dealt with and ideas ready by market opening. Most brokers are at their desk until 5:00 or 6:00 P.M., finishing up paperwork for the day's transactions and preparing a list of ideas and clients to call in the morning.

Successful brokers are not order-takers—they actively solicit their clients' transactions, calling with ideas for securities to buy and sell and other investment ideas that meet the client's objectives and needs.

Sometimes new recruits are concerned that they'll have to compromise their ethical or moral values in order to be a successful Account Executive. This is fortunately not the case, although it takes most brokers some time and trial before learning what style is both effective for them and consistent with their code of business ethics.

Stockbrokers rarely travel extensively. Occasional trips to the home office are all that most brokers undertake, although some travel frequently by car to visit clients.

Sex and the Stockbroker

There is no reason why a woman cannot be as successful as a stockbroker as a man. Client acceptance of women is high: often, little old ladies prefer to deal with men, but the highest officers of the biggest corporations are happy dealing with a woman. Often, they prefer it.

Individuals who have reached these levels of achievement have such confidence in themselves that their ego does not demand that they dump on anyone. They rely on their judgment of who knows what she is talking about, and who does not. These men often work with female bankers, investment bankers and attorneys, and have come to value the thorough preparation and attention to detail in which professional women often outshine their male colleagues. Top executives appreciate having this level of service dedicated to their personal brokerage business.

Being a woman is still a problem in getting hired. Old prejudices die hard on Wall Street, and this one is still going strong in Sales Managers' offices. They have usually seen too many female applicants who don't understand the nature of the job—who think it's finance and economics, not sales. A broker doesn't spend her time doing research or being a financial planner, she spends it making cold calls. Women who understand everything discussed in this chapter can get hired. Read the "Suggested Reading" at the end of this chapter for even more flavor of a broker's life. Then head for the Sales Manager's office to mount a determined, polite but persistent, campaign to begin your career as a stockbroker.

What Do Brokers Earn?

Starting salaries are traditionally low ($15,000 to $25,000) because brokerage firms want to hire trainees who know beyond all doubt that this is the job they want, are willing to make a sacrifice to get it, and are hungry to earn more by generating commissions as soon as possible.

At the major firms, the average broker in 1984 earned in excess of $80,000. It's not unusual for a first-year broker to earn $50,000; many earn more than $30,000. There are thousands of brokers who earn in excess of $100,000, hundreds who earn more than $300,000, and a dozen or so who earn $1 million or more a year.

Why Become a Stockbroker?

A salesman is got to dream, boy.
It comes with the territory.
—Arthur Miller (Death of a Salesman)

The number one reason to become a stockbroker is money. The number two reason is freedom. A stockbroker is an entrepreneur, with the freedom to decide how much money to earn and how to earn it. Many $100,000-plus-a-year brokers didn't even go to college, much less earn an M.B.A. degree.

Unlike many other salespeople, a stockbroker has no fixed territory. Where do you go after you've sold copy machines to all the businesses in your territory? A stockbroker does not have that problem—there are millions of people within reach of the phone who are potential clients.

A broker's income is limited only by the limits he or she chooses, not by salary ranges established by a corporate Personnel office. The income is not subject to wage-price freezes, either national or company. You decide how many hours will be in your working day, and whether you want to work nights and weekends.

Freedom means choosing the clients with whom you want to work and, even more important, those with whom you don't want to work. You may choose which products and services to sell. You may decide to specialize in such areas as options or tax shelters, or you may sell fifty different products. You decide whether your approach is hard sell or soft sell. Brokers are also independent from managers in most ways. A manager can be a great help, but can do little to stand in your way. You can usually ignore a manager you don't like without penalty to your earnings or your future—a luxury few jobs can offer.

Brokers bear the risk of failure but have the gratification of seeing results and getting paid for their work almost immediately. There are no annual bonuses decided upon by somebody else. You see the bottom line—your paycheck—every month.

Why Not Become a Stockbroker?

The almost-constant rejection experienced by brokers prospecting for new clients is unbearable for many new brokers. Call after call, trying to talk with people who are essentially happy without you can be trying. Hardly anyone really likes prospecting, but for some it is torture. Yet a broker cannot be successful without a continuous prospecting program.

Some stockbrokers burn out early because they have been too aggressive in dealing with their clients. Too many client complaints, lost accounts, and potential legal problems can cause burnout.

Although most successful brokers stay in the business for many years, it's possible to become tired or discouraged about the relentness need to prospect. Once a broker stops working hard, less success will almost inevitably follow, and can cause the broker to leave the business.

Market cycles take their toll. Recommending securities that eventually lose substantial sums of money for valued clients can be discouraging for any broker. If the stock market is weak for too long, the discouragement can be fatal.

Competition from discount brokerage firms, including banks, has made it more difficult for brokers in full-service firms to justify their higher commission charges to their clients. In addition, electronic technology now permits discount brokerage firm clients to "execute" purchases and sales directly from their personal computer, a trend that may take even more business away from the full-service brokers.

In order to keep their commissions competitive, the full-service firms must reduce their costs of doing business. A few of these firms are doing this by paying some retail brokers a salary rather than commission, a trend that some in the industry feel will continue. If so, the earnings potential of the retail Account Executive may be diminished.

At some firms, pressure on brokers to produce certain minimum levels of commissions is creating broker dissatisfaction. More and more, brokerage firms are emphasizing that poor producers cannot count on their jobs.

The rules for brokers on the way up are, however, the same as they have always been: work hard, work legally, and don't quit. The best and biggest firms bend over backwards to give their brokers the training and sales support they need. As long as you keep working hard, there is nothing to stop you from joining the superstar brokers who generate one million dollars or more in commissions each year.

What Kind of Person Are They Looking For?

Many firms hire people directly from college or graduate school. Others require some work experience, usually in sales. Most of the largest require a college degree, but some can still be persuaded to hire a non-college graduate with stellar sales experience. Only a few firms require an M.B.A. or even view it as a plus in retail sales, although most require the degree for institutional sales.

Sales experience is always a plus for getting hired as a stockbroker. The best sales experience is in financial services, but office-equipment, ethical-drug, printing, and advertising salespeople are all strong candidates. In good markets such as that of 1983, teachers, pro athletes, bankers, and even M.D.'s were being hired as retail brokers!

Often, a brokerage firm's Sales Manager will try to convince an applicant that the position of Sales Assistant is a steppingstone to a position as an Account Executive. This is rarely true. There are some strong prejudices in the brokerage community. This is one of them. Occasionally, an extremely talented, self-starting dynamo will manage to convince the Sales Manager that he or she should be promoted to Account Executive—but, even when this is done, the level of support given to the individual may be minimal. As a Sales Manager once explained to me, "when an S.A. insists that she wants to become a broker, I say yes, give her a phone and a desk and let her fail." Don't let yourself be talked into taking this position if what you really want is to be a broker. Keep trying—approach every office of every firm in town and don't take no for an answer.

How to Apply

Try to join one of the large, financial supermarket firms. Their training programs are outstanding, and they offer a great deal of ongoing support to their sales force.

Branch offices do their own hiring, so your application should be directed to the Sales Managers of as many branches of as many firms as you have the energy to pursue.

It's quite common for applicants to be routinely rejected on the first round of application. Because polite persistence in the face of rejection is a necessary quality for successful stockbrokers, many managers will talk only to those persistent enough to keep calling two or three or more times to try to arrange an interview.

Suggested Reading

John Andrew, "If 'Cold Calls' Freeze Brokers' Spirit, They Can Warm to the Job," *The Wall Street Journal*, March 9, 1984.

Barbara Ettore, "Don't let the slam dunks get to you'", *Forbes*, July 18, 1983.

Richard L. Stern, "Look at the brokers' yachts," *Forbes*, January 17, 1983.

The Institutional Account Executive

The function of an Institutional Account Executive is quite different from that of a Retail Account Executive. An Institutional A/E functions primarily as a liaison between institutional clients and the brokerage firm's research department. Research analysts and portfolio managers from institutions—primarily mutual funds, bank trust departments, and pension fund managers—rely extensively on research supplied to them by the brokerage firms. The institutions then "pay" for the most useful research by buying stocks and bonds through the brokerage firms that supply them with it.

The Institutional Account Executive assigned to the account of a mutual fund makes sure that the brokerage firm's research analysts are communicating with the research analysts at the fund. When the brokerage analysts change their opinion or earnings estimates on a stock, the institutional broker calls the clients immediately, telling them of the change. The brokerage analysts also visit the institutional clients regularly, either in one-on-one meetings with the larger funds or in large luncheon meetings to which a number of institutional investors are invited.

The institutional broker's goal is to maximize the commissions generated by the transactions—purchases and sales of securities—executed in the institutional clients' accounts. This is done both by promoting the firm's research and by encouraging them to buy securities recommended by the firm. Unlike a retail broker, who has a virtually unlimited universe of potential clients, the institutional broker is assigned clients to develop and service.

An institutional broker is freed almost entirely from the relentless prospecting required of the retail broker, but may "prospect" by trying to develop accounts with institutional investors who have not previously been clients of the firm.

A retail broker almost always has the luxury of choosing areas in which to specialize—certain stocks, certain industries, or even non-stock investments such as bonds or tax shelters. The institutional broker, on the other hand, mut be thoroughly familiar with all areas of the firm's equity research and the research analysts' opinions on all of the stocks they follow, which can number in the thousands. Where a new retail broker spends nights and weekends prospecting, a new institutional broker spends countless hours reading and studying research reports.

These brokers do a great deal of entertaining— lunch, dinner, squash, sporting events—both to get to know their clients in order to better serve their needs, and to help set themselves apart from the competition. Fast and accurate delivery of important research information is vital to an institutional broker's success, but Raiders tickets don't hurt!

Commissions charged to institutional investors are heavily discounted, but even so, Institutional Account Executives have enjoyed substantial incomes. Projections for growth in institutional business, due largely to growth in all kinds of retirement plans, from Individual Retirement Accounts (IRA's) for individuals (which are often invested in mutual funds) to retirement plans of corporations, are enormous. The degree to which this growth will translate into increased opportunity for institutional brokers is, however, questionable.

At the same time that brokerage firms are becoming more aware of the high cost of delivering the research "product" to institutional investors via Institutional Account Executives, technological advances are making it possible for more direct contact between institutional clients and the brokerage firms' research analysts. Electronic technology has made it possible for analysts to "publish" their research opinions in electronic media immediately accessible by their clients. Videoconferencing permits "face-to-face" meetings between analyst and client. These innovations provide for a more efficient relationship between institutions and analysts, but effectively bypass the institutional broker. Some in the industry feel that the continuation of this trend will make Institutional Account Executives less important to their firms as the analyst, rather than the broker, becomes more and more the key person influencing the client's decision of which brokerage firm to choose for executing transactions. As a result, opportunities for individuals to begin careers as Institutional A/E's are limited.

For those few positions that are available, an M.B.A. degree is almost always required. Ideal candidates are hard-working, self-starting, ambitious, intelligent, and articulate. Earnings potential is dramatic: most institutional brokers are earning in excess of $100,000 after five years in the business, with some top salespeople earning as much as $500,000. There are, however, already indications that some brokerage firms are taking steps to improve profitability by changing formulas under which institutional brokers are paid. These changes may translate into lower earnings for these salespeople in the future.

As with retail brokers, individual branch offices do their own hiring. Apply to the Office Manager of the Institutional Office or Department.

Other Positions at Brokerage Firms

In addition to positions in Investment Banking (including Sales and Trading) and Research, discussed in Chapters 7 and 9, brokerage firms hire entry-level professionals in Operations Management, Computer Systems, and in other management-development programs.

Operations Management

Most major brokerage firms offer training programs in Operations Management—cashiering operations (taking in deposits of money and securities), bookkeeping, securities transfers between firms (from seller to buyer), order entry, execution of orders on the exchange floors, confirmation of transactions, and many other areas.

These are management, not sales positions. Individuals who do well can advance rapidly within the firm. Often, frequent relocation is among the requirements for upward mobility in Operations Management within large brokerage firms. Taking advantage of the next move up may require a move to another city rather than waiting for an opening to develop in your home town.

Successful Operations Managers are outstanding communicators. Their job is to manage the smooth functioning of operations, which means managing people; to take on the many problems that can result from the massive volume of securities transactions they process and resolve them to the satisfaction of the customer, the Account Executive, and the firm—often an extremely difficult task.

These are not entrepreneurial careers, and as such do not offer the sky-high salaries seen in other Wall Street positions. Nor do they demand the long days and nights required of investment bankers, research analysts, and Account Executives.

Generally, positions in these training programs are filled at the home office, through the College Relations office of Personnel.

Management Development Programs

The Appendix of this book lists several large brokerage firms that offer management development programs in areas other than those discussed above. For example, Merrill Lynch's Corporate Intern Program offers a small and highly-select group of college graduates the opportunity to work in several different areas within the firm (Capital Markets, Securities Research, and others) and the opportunity to interact with management at all levels.

Such programs offer outstanding opportunities for training in the securities industry. Generally, they last from one to two years but, unlike Financial Analyst programs in investment banking, are designed not to precede business school but to launch you directly on a career in the area of your choice within the firm.

Generally, the College Relations group within Personnel handles hiring for these training programs.

Chapter 9

Securities Research Analysis

*Research is a way of life
dedicated to discovery.
—Anonymous*

What Do Securities Research Analysts Do?

SECURITIES RESEARCH ANALYSTS study stocks and bonds in order to make recommendations on which ones to buy and sell. While the majority of analysts follow only stocks (*equities*), others specialize in bonds or other *fixed-income securities*. Bond analysts try to determine which bonds offer the best combination of safety and high return from both interest income and potential capital gain.

Most equity analysts follow companies and their stocks by industry. Most analysts for brokerage firms today follow twenty to thirty companies within one or two industry groups. Some analysts, such as those who follow utility stocks, may cover more than one hundred companies.

Research analysts strive to learn everything there is to know about the companies and industries they follow: their history, management, products, markets, competition, and, most importantly, finances. An analyst studies past results in order to project future prospects. One key product of an analyst's research is an estimate of future earnings. An analyst is judged on how close that estimate is to the numbers the company actually earns.

The work is heavily quantitative. Research analysts must scrutinize the financial statements of corporations in minute detail. They must be conversant with every nuance of accounting rules, both proposed and current. Today, analysts use computers extensively to crunch the extensive financial data they analyze and to prepare the *spread-sheet* statements used for comparison of financial and technical information about securities.

The primary factor determining analysts' success is the accuracy of their judgment of whether a stock should be bought, held, or sold. For example, an analyst following the restaurant and lodging industry is responsible for maintaining, at all times, a "buy," "hold," or "sell" opinion on each of the twenty or so stocks followed. An analyst who upgrades an opinion on McDonald's from "hold" to "buy" just prior to a major advance in the stock is a hero; if, on the other hand, the opinion change was from "hold" to "sell," the analyst will be regarded as a loser.

Research analysts do a tremendous amount of writing. Today it is impossible to be considered a first-rate analyst without producing frequent, comprehensive research reports on companies and industries followed. If writing is not one of your skills, or if you hate doing it, banish the thought of a career as a securities analyst.

Research analysts are employed by just about every kind of financial firm: bank trust departments, brokerage firm research departments, mutual funds, insurance companies, and others. Virtually any institution investing in common stocks requires securities analysts. Depending on the type of firm, analysts make their recommendations to portfolio managers, brokers, or directly to clients. As discussed in "The Institutional Account Executive" in Chapter 8, "Securities Brokerage," today the analyst is responsible more and more for the sales aspect of institutional brokerage. The relationship of research analysts to portfolio managers is further discussed in "Trust" in Chapter 6, "Commercial Banking."

Analysts at brokerage firms may have great power: a change in their opinion on a company can cause the stock to rise or fall as much as three or four dollars per share a day, as institutional investors respond to their recommendation and begin to buy or sell the stock.

Research analysts at brokerage firms are public figures within the financial community. Their opinions are widely sought and frequently published by major financial publications reporting on the companies and industries they follow.

Once a year, *Institutional Investor* magazine polls institutional clients on their choices of the best research analysts. Bank trust departments, mutual funds, and other institutional investors indicate by name the analysts whose advice has been most valuable to them. The magazine publishes the names of the winners as the "All-America Research Team" in the October issue. For each industry group, first, second, and third place winners are named and pictured, and a list of runners-up is printed. Over three hundred analysts from more than thirty firms are named. These are the "All-Star" analysts who have combined excellent written research not only with good ideas and good timing, but also with effective marketing of their ideas.

The results of this poll can make or break an analyst. Firms such as Merrill Lynch that routinely place high in the overall rankings are rumored to offer salaries as high as $500,000 for top-place finishers.

Research analysts spend a great deal of time traveling. They visit the companies they follow regularly, as well as attending conventions and trade shows. Sell-side analysts employed by brokerage firms spend a lot of time meeting with institutional clients. An analyst's hours are long, the work is challenging, and the unpredictability of the stock market can make it frustrating. An analyst may have prepared an outstanding fundamental analysis of a company's prospects, predicting strong growth in earnings, and assigning a "buy" recommendation to the stock, yet a negative stock market may force the stock down with all the others. As one analyst put it, "in this business, if you're right 55% of the time, you're doing well; 60%, you're a hero."

> *(The stock market is) a Falstaffian joke*
> *that frequently degenerates into a madhouse.*
> —Benjamin Graham

Analysts' compensation depends on the type of institution for which they work. It is generally in line with that of other professionals within their firm. Many companies pay analysts on a bonus system that allows them to earn more if their ideas are successful. Starting salaries for B.A.'s are $15,000 to $30,000 plus bonus; M.B.A. starting salaries are from $30,000 to $50,000 plus bonus. Mutual fund Vice Presidents who have been in the business five years may earn $50,000 to $150,000 plus bonuses in good years.

The Charter Financial Analyst Program

The Financial Analysts' Federation sponsors the Charter Financial Analyst (C.F.A.) Program, which accredits securities analysts. Most mutual funds, investment counseling firms, and bank trust departments now either require or strongly urge research analysts and portfolio managers to earn the C.F.A. designation. For those who have launched a career in securities research without an M.B.A. degree, the C.F.A. credential is especially important, since many in the industry regard the C.F.A. program as equally or even more significant.

In order to obtain your charter and be entitled to the C.F.A. designation (as in "John Smith, C.F.A."), you must complete three rigorous examinations. Since the exams are given only once a year, it takes three years to obtain a charter. These are not multiple-choice, but exhaustive essay examinations requiring careful study of many volumes of preparatory material. Even those with years of experience in the business must really study to pass these tests. Knowledge of accounting, economics, the securities markets, and other areas critical to financial analysis are tested in the C.F.A. examinations.

How Do You Get a Job as a Research Analyst?

Apply for a position as a Research Assistant with bank trust departments and research departments of brokerage firms. These types of firms are the most likely to hire inexperienced people without an M.B.A. degree at an entry level. Other firms employing research analysts are mutual funds, investment counseling firms, institutional research "boutiques" providing only research services for a fee, and large corporations that manage their own pension and profit-sharing retirement plans. Many of these firms are listed in the Appendix of this book; the *Money Market Directory* (see "Resources") lists others.

In contacting brokerage firms for a position as a Research Assistant, write to individual analysts heading up industry groups as well as the Director of Research and Personnel. To find analysts' names, use your contacts, ask the secretary of the Director of Research for a list, consult the *Money Market Directory*, or check the October issue of *Institutional Investor*.

Don't overlook the possibility of starting as a securities analyst with financial services or publications, such as Moody's Investor Service, Dun & Bradstreet, or Standard & Poor's Corporation (see "Resources"). These organizations rate the creditworthiness of corporations and government borrowers. Their ratings are widely observed and respected. Value Line, Inc., publishes the widely-read subscription publication *The Value Line Investment Survey*. They also hire and train many analysts each year.

Suggested Reading

"The All-America Research Team," *Institutional Investor*, October, 1984.

Go to a branch office of a brokerage firm and ask for some samples of research reports written by their analysts.

Chapter 10

Investment Counseling

INVESTMENT COUNSELING firms are securities managers. They manage money for institutions and individuals in virtually the same way as has already been described under "Trust" in Chapter 6, "Commercial Banking." In 1983, these institutions managed some $781 billion dollars in tax-exempt (retirement) funds alone!

In addition to their portfolio management activities, many investment counseling firms, such as Scudder, Stevens, and Clark and Putnam Management Company, also manage mutual funds. Primary financial professional positions in these firms are those of Portfolio Manager and Research Analyst, with opportunities also in Operations and Computer Systems.

Salaries earned by professionals in investment counseling firms tend to be comparable to or, in many cases, higher than those earned by commercial bankers. After ten years, Research Analysts or Portfolio Managers may earn $50,000 to $150,000.

As with bank trust departments, performance matters in today's competitive environment. Those who make money for their clients and attract new clients will be compensated accordingly.

Although most firms hire only M.B.A.'s, some hire B.A.'s. Occasionally there are opportunities for an enterprising Administrative Assistant to work up to a position as a Junior Analyst. In general, however, these firms are not the most likely to offer entry-level positions; it's better to start with an apprenticeship in a bank or brokerage firm. While there, you can begin to work on attaining the C.F.A. charter and greatly enhance your opportunities for a later move to an investment counseling firm.

Chapter 11

Mutual Funds

I buy low and sell high.
—*Bernard Baruch*

MUTUAL FUNDS provide professional money management to individuals and institutions investing either relatively small or large amounts of money. In a mutual fund, pools of money are collected and invested.

In order to invest in a mutual fund, an investor buys shares in the fund. For their professional investment services, the mutual fund may charge the purchaser a commission when they buy shares. All charge an annual management fee.

Mutual fund companies are structured similarly to bank trust departments and investment counseling firms. See "Trust" in Chapter 6, "Commercial Banking" and Chapter 10, "Investment Counseling" for a full description of their functions. Many mutual funds are in fact managed by investment counseling firms.

Each mutual fund has a stated objective: for example, aggressive growth. The objective helps investors determine which fund is most suitable for them, and guides the investment decisions of the managers.

Each fund has one or more fund managers who make the investment decisions. The fund managers' role is analogous to that of a Portfolio Manager in a bank trust department or investment counseling firm. Their decisions are influenced by the recommendations of the Research Analysts regarding which stocks should be bought and sold, and may be further guided by an Investment Committee.

Mutual funds often employ a sizeable sales and marketing staff to sell the funds to the public. They design brochures, plan advertisements, and outline strategies for marketing to both individuals and institutional investors.

Salary levels and recommendations for obtaining entry-level positions are the same as those given for investment counseling firms.

The Appendix lists many investment counseling and mutual fund companies. For the names, addresses, and phone numbers of others, consult Wiesenberger's *Investment Companies* (see "Resources").

Suggested Reading

See *Forbes* magazine's annual mutual fund issue (August 27 1984).

Read Wiesenberger's *Investment Companies* (see "Resources") for articles about the industry as well as information on specific companies.

Chapter 12

Insurance Companies

---

*Insurance is an ingenious modern game of chance
in which the player is permitted to enjoy the
comfortable conviction that he is beating
the man who keeps the table.*
—Ambrose Bierce

MOST JOB SEEKERS do not really understand the function of insurance companies. They know that insurance salespeople sell life insurance, annuities, and property and casualty insurance, but do not realize that the primary business of an insurance company is investment.

Premiums on insurance policies constitute vast sums of money paid in to insurance companies. Much of this money will not be paid out for many years. Thus, these firms are major institutional investors in the equity and fixed-income markets, as well as in other areas such as real estate, mortgages, and even venture capital. They employ research analysts in these specific areas as well as in general economic research. The role of analysts in the financial markets is described in the chapter on "Securities Research Analysis."

Investment Divisions of insurance companies hire many research analysts in these areas each year. Most of the major companies require or strongly prefer M.B.A.'s, although some do occasionally hire B.A.'s.

Insurance companies also employ large numbers of salespeople to market and sell their products and services. The old stereotype of the insurance salesman going from door to door no longer applies. Today, insurance salespeople are trained in marketing sophisticated financial vehicles to individuals, corporations, and other institutional investors.

Many financial planners have their roots in insurance sales. These planners work with individuals to help them formulate a comprehensive plan for managing their assets—minimizing income and estate taxes, planning and executing Wills and Trusts, planning for their retirement and their childrens' college educations, as well as determining their insurance needs. Generally, they work for a fixed fee—either a flat sum that is determined according to the complexity of the client's situation, or an hourly rate. In order to offer the client advice untainted by any conflict of interest, many do not sell any products for which they receive a commission.

Insurance companies are now expanding aggressively in the arena of financial services. Prudential-Bache Securities is developing a fully-integrated approach to the sale of insurance and brokerage products and services. Other major brokerage firms also have insurance subsidiaries.

Insurance companies have extraordinary record-keeping requirements and process immense volumes of paperwork and data. Accordingly, they are among the largest users of data processing services in the country, and often offer outstanding training programs in computer systems. These are generally offered at their headquarters office. Large numbers of college graduates with B.A. and B.S. degrees are hired for these programs. Previous experience with computer processing is a plus, but not a necessity.

For those B.A.'s with majors in mathematics, insurance companies offer excellent actuarial training programs. Actuaries provide the sophisticated models employed by insurance companies to determine the statistical likelihood of death or catastrophe, and thus the premiums that should be charged for policies. Their career path may lead to management or the investment division, where actuaries may apply their quantitative skills to models for theoretical financial analysis such as Modern Portfolio Theory.

On the investment side, salaries for insurance companies are comparable to those of commercial bankers—Vice Presidents may make $50,000 to $100,000 after five to ten years. Apply to the head of the investment division in the headquarters office.

For sales positions, you should apply to each insurance company branch office and check also with the headquarters office to see whether they do any centralized hiring. Both the work and the qualifications required are similar to those discussed in Chapter 8, "Securities Brokerage."

If you are interested in the field of financial planning, the best source of company names is the Yellow Pages (look under "Financial Planning Consultants").

Chapter 13

Venture Capital

*We are all in the gutter,
but some of us are looking at the stars.*
—Oscar Wilde

VENTURE CAPITAL is one of the financial hot spots of the 1980's. These small firms provide money to young, growing companies—from "seed money" for the development of an idea from scratch to first, second, or third round financing.

The firms they finance are privately held—their stock is not available for purchase by the general public. In return for their early investment, the venture capital investors receive stock in the company. They expect to sell the stock at a profit when the company goes public in one to five years.

Venture capital investors can expect an investment in a growing company to return up to ten times their money if successful. They also expect that many of the ventures in which they invest will fail. In addition to investing in the company, the venture investors will take a seat on its Board of Directors in order to influence the decisions of the firm. The business is extraordinarily high risk, high return. It is not for the faint of heart.

Some venture capital firms such as L.F. Rothschild, Unterberg, Towbin and Hambrecht & Quist are also major-bracket investment banking firms. They not only invest in companies at an early stage but also manage their initial public and subsequent stock offerings.

Venture capital firms tend to be located near the spawning grounds of technology. Leaders such as Arthur Rock, Hambrecht & Quist, and Kleiner, Perkin, Caulfield & Byers are in San Francisco (an hour north of Silicon Valley). T.A. Associates and

Greylock Management are in Boston, not far from Route 128, the heart of that high-technology region.

The multimillion-dollar sums earned by venture capital partners from their successful investments have attracted large numbers of would-be entrants to the business. Yet venture capital firms remain a small, close-knit community. This chapter is short because, even with an M.B.A. degree, it is difficult to obtain one of the rare entry-level positions, and it is practically impossible for anyone without the degree to enter the field.

The Appendix lists a number of venture capital firms. Others are listed in *Pratt's Guide to Venture Capital Sources* and other directories (see "Resources").

Suggested Reading

Alexander Taylor III, "Making a Mint Overnight," *Time*, January 23, 1984.

Part III

Conclusion, or The End of the Beginning

Chapter 14

Your Wall Street Career Begins Today

Now, this is not the end.
It is not even the beginning of the end.
But it is, perhaps, the end of the beginning.
—*Winston Churchill*

THE KNOWLEDGE YOU'VE GAINED from reading this book gives you a tremendous head start on the competition. You know what your goal is, you can picture yourself achieving it, and the action plan you must implement to reach that goal is in place. Begin today to execute that plan.

You know that your success in landing a job on Wall Street depends upon neither your credentials nor your connections, but on the kind of effort you apply. Your action plan includes network building and a program to ensure that you prepare thoroughly for every interview. You are prepared to be enthusiastic, confident, and knowledgeable as you meet with representatives of many firms. You are committed to follow up on every interview and opportunity. Most of all, you know that your winning attitude will be in place throughout your career search, the attitude of a winner on Wall Street.

138

Thank God life may be always so full
of new beginnings that it never need
be stale to any of us.
—Phillips Brooks

Part IV

Resources

Notes

As there are now equal opportunities for both men and women on Wall Street, this book is for both sexes. The writing is intended to be non-sexist, not sexless. Suggestions in Casey Miller and Kate Swift's *The Handbook of Nonsexist Writing* have been used; and terms such as "he/she," "alumna/alumnus," and the use of sex-specific names in examples ("John Smith/Rebecca Smith") have been alternated.

Chapter 1, *Setting Your Sights on Success*

See "Executive compensation: The top 50," *Financial World*, May 30-June 12, 1984. Source: Sibson & Company.

Chapter 5, *Evolution in Financial Services*

See Roger L. Jenkins, Richard C. Reizenstein, and F. G. Rodgers, "Probing Opinions: Report Cards on the MBA," *Harvard Business Review*, September-October 1984. From a survey of *Fortune* "500" executives, business school deans, and faculty, authors conclude that "neither executives nor academics are satisfied, for example, with the way that current MBA graduates write and speak." Also: "when it comes to written work . . . more than half the business respondents express dissatisfaction."

Chapter 6, *Commercial Banking*

See *American Banker*, 6/28/84, for rankings of trust managers.

Resources

Directories

Financial Analysts Federation Directory. Annual. Lists all securities research analysts who are members of this organization, cross-referenced by firm (with name, address, and phone number). Available from FAF members.

Guide to Venture Capital Sources. Ed: Stanley E. Pratt, Wellesley, Massachusetts: Venture Economics, 8th ed., April 1984. Available in business libraries. Contains interesting information about the venture capital business as well as a thorough directory of venture capital firms.

Money Market Directory of Pension Funds and their Investment Managers. Annual. Ed: T. H. Fitzgerald, Jr. Money Market Directories, Inc., 300 East Market St., Charlottesville VA 22901, 804-977-1450. Lists investment managers and analysts by industry. Available in business libraries and some public libraries.

Moody's Bank & Finance Manual. Annual. Moody's Investor Service, 99 Church St., New York NY 10007, 212-553-0300 (subsidiary of Dun & Bradstreet). Exhaustive information about banks. Available in business libraries and many public libraries. Also in branch offices of brokerage firms.

Wiesenberger Investment Companies Service, *Investment Companies.* Annual. Wiesenberger Financial Services, 1633 Broadway, New York NY 10019, 212-977-7453. Lists names, addresses, phone numbers, and extensive information about mutual fund companies. Available in business libraries, some public libraries, and branch offices of brokerage firms.

Louis Engel and Brendan Boyd, *How to Buy Stocks.* New York, NY: Bantam Books. 7th Edition (paperback).

Michael Korda, *Success!*, New York, NY: Random House, 1977.

John T. Molloy, *Dress for Success*, New York NY: P. H. Wyden, 1975.

Periodicals

Institutional Investor, see especially October 1984 issue, "The All-America Research Team."

Investment Publications

Standard & Poor's Stock Reports. Standard & Poor's Corporation, 25 Broadway, New York NY 10004, 212-924-6825. Loose-leaf, brief one-page research reports on all NYSE and ASE stocks and most OTC stocks. Available in business libraries, many public libraries, and branch offices of brokerage firms.

The Value Line Investment Survey. Value Line, Inc., 711 Third Ave., New York, NY 10017, 212-687-3965. Research reports prepared by securities analysts on thousands of listed stocks. Available in business libraries and many public libraries.

Appendix

500 Financial Firms

Information in this Appendix is designed to permit you to launch your job hunt easily and thoroughly from your own desk, sparing you hours in the Placement Office/Career Center or Library Reference Room. Addresses and phone numbers listed are those of the Personnel or Recruiting area to which you should direct your inquiries. It's still a good idea to call first and find out the precise name of the program you're interested in (is it the "Loan Officer Development Program" or the "Managerial Lending Program"?) and verify their specific requirements (such as an Accounting major or an M.B.A. degree).

Information included herein was compiled during November, 1985, for those seeking jobs in 1986. Although efforts have been made to verify this information, no representation is made as to its accuracy or completeness. It's always a good idea to call and make sure that you are contacting the correct person.

Certain abbreviations have been used in this list. In your letters, be sure to spell out all abbreviations that are part of names or titles.

Nat'l.	= National
Pers.	= Personnel
Dir.	= Director
Bancorp.	= Bancorporation
	(where "Bancorp" is not followed by a period, it should not be written out)
Corp.	= Corporation
Dept.	= Department
Mgmt.	= Management
Exec.	= Executive
Rep.	= Representative
sub.	= subsidiary
cont.	= controlled
Bldg.	= Building

Banks

Banks are listed in alphabetical order by name of bank holding company followed by rank in the *Business Week* "Bank Score-board" of April 8, 1985, which lists the 200 largest bank holding companies ranked by assets as of 12/31/84. For example, the entry

> CBT Corporation #54

denotes that CBT Corporation is the 54th largest bank holding company according to the *Business Week* survey. Where no ranking number is indicated, the bank was not included in the *Business Week* list.

Where a bank trust department or bank subsidiary manages substantial assets, that is denoted by an asterisk (*). For example,

> American Fletcher Corp. #105
> *American Fletcher Bank

denotes that American Fletcher Bank's trust department is among the largest in the industry (with over $1 billion under management).

The top twenty bank trust departments are denoted by two asterisks (**). For example,

> AmeriTrust Corp. #55
> **AmeriTrust Company

The designation of banks with large trust departments is significant for those seeking a career as a Research Analyst or Portfolio Manager, rather than in commercial lending or other areas of banking.

Where the name of a bank subsidiary of a bank holding company is listed, applicants should direct their letter to the subsidiary, not the holding company. For example, in the entry

> Liberty United Bancorp, Inc.
> Liberty Nat'l Bank and Trust Company of Louisville
> Paul Corrington

applicants should direct their letter to Liberty National Bank and Trust Company of Louisville, not Liberty United Bancorp.

For explanation of "*" or "**" see above discussion.

Affiliated Bankshares of
    Colorado, Inc. #144
Ms. Barbara Muntyan
Dir. of Personnel
1101 Arapahoe Ave.
Boulder CO 80302
303-449-2030

First Nat'l Bank of
    Colorado Springs
Ms. Dorothy Robbins
Personnel Office
P.O. Box 1699
Colorado Springs CO 80942
303-471-5000

Allied Bancshares, Inc. #36
Allied Bank of Texas
Personnel Dept.
P.O. Box 3326
Houston TX 77253
713-226-1666

The Amalgamated Bank of
    New York
Mr. Thomas Del Core
Personnel Department
11-15 Union Square
New York NY 10003
212-255-6200

American Fletcher Corp. #105
*American Fletcher Bank
Personnel Division
108 No. Pennsylvania St.
Indianapolis IN 46277
317-639-7987

**American National Bank
    & Trust Co. #99
(acq. by First Chicago)
Mr. Ronald Yenerich
Personnel Dept.
33 North LaSalle St.
Chicago IL 60690
312-661-6907

American Security Corp. #92
*American Security Bank
Mr. Roy Daugherty
Executive Recruiter
635 Massachusetts Ave. NW
Washington, D.C. 20001
202-624-4100

AmeriTrust Corp. #55
**AmeriTrust Company
Mrs. Sharon Lebovitz
Vice President
900 Euclid Ave.
Cleveland OH 44101
216-687-5000

AmSouth Bancorporation #85
AmSouth Bank
Mr. Sonny Pritchett
Personnel Dept.
P.O. Box 11007
Birmingham AL 35288
205-326-5447

Arizona Bancwest Corp. #114
The Arizona Bank
Human Resources Dept.
101 N. 1st Ave.
Phoenix AZ 85003
602-262-2000

Atlantic Bancorporation #102
(to be acq. by First Union)
Atlantic Nat'l Bank of Florida
Mr. Andy Hendersen
Employment Manager
General Mail Center
Jacksonville FL 32231
904-632-6802

BanCal Tri-State Corp.
(sub. of Mitsubishi Bank)
The Bank of California
400 California St.
San Francisco CA 94104
415-765-0400

Banco de Ponce #184
(Ponce, Puerto Rico)
Personnel Dept.
10 Rockefeller Plaza
New York NY 10020
212-247-3355

BancOklahoma Corp. #118
Bank of Oklahoma
Ms. Renate Hucke
P.O. Box 2300
Tulsa OK 74192
918-588-6578

Banc One Corporation #38
Bank One Trust Co.
Human Resources Services
100 East Broad St.
Columbus OH 43271-0161
614-463-5984

Banco Popular
   de Puerto Rico #107
Banco Popular Center
Hato Rey
Personnel Department
P.O. Box 2708
San Juan PR 00936
450 7th Ave.
New York NY 10123
212-868-4747

Bancorp Hawaii, Inc. #98
Bank of Hawaii
Employment
P.O. Box 2900
Honolulu HI 96846
808-537-8111

BancTEXAS Group Inc. #172
BancTEXAS Dallas
Human Resources Dept.
P.O. Box 2249
Dallas TX 75221
214-969-6214

BankAmerica Corporation #2
*Bank of America
Mr. Jack Van Berkel
College Relations
Dept. 3616
P.O. Box 37000
San Francisco CA 94137
415-953-6273
*Also BA Investment Mgmt.
   Corp.

Bank of Boston Corporation #16
**First Nat'l Bank of Boston
College Relations Dept.
P.O. Box 1928
Boston MA 02105
617-434-2138

Bankers Trust New York
   Corp. #9
**Bankers Trust Company
Management Recruiting
   Department
280 Park Ave.
Floor 2 West
New York NY 10017
212-850-1589

Bankers Trust of
   South Carolina #181
(to be acq. by NCNB Corp.)
Mrs. Debbe Chakales
Office of Recruitment and
   Personnel
P.O. Box 448
1301 Gervais St.
Columbia SC 29202
803-771-2167

Bank Leumi Le-Israel B.M. #138
Personnel Dept.
100 No. LaSalle St.
Chicago IL 60602
312-781-1800
579 Fifth Ave.
New York NY 10017
212-382-4000

Bank of New England Corp. #57
Bank of New England
Ms. Donna Baughman
Management Recruitment
28 State St.
Boston MA 02109
617-722-6426

The Bank of New York
   Company, Inc. #26
*The Bank of New York
Mr. Thomas Angers
Personnel Dept.
48 Wall St.
New York NY 10015
212-530-8609

Bank Shares #194
Marquette Bank Minneapolis
Human Resources Department
6th & Marquette
Minneapolis MN 55480
612-341-5757

Banks of Iowa, Inc. #182
Personnel
520 Walnut
Des Moines IA 50306
515-245-6320

Bank South Corp. #148
Ms. Jane Callaway
Human Resources - 8
P.O. Box 5092
Atlanta GA 30302
404-529-4296

Bank of Tokyo Trust Co. #78
(cont. by Bank of Tokyo Ltd.)
Human Resources Dept.
100 Broadway
New York NY 10005
212-766-3400

Bank of Virginia Company #90
Bank of Virginia
Mr. Gregg Paul
Management Recruitment Officer
P.O. Box 25970
Richmond VA 23260
804-747-2000

Barnett Banks of Florida, Inc. #29
Personnel Dept.
100 Laura St.
Jacksonville FL 40789
904-791-7720

Baybanks, Inc. #75
BayBank Middlesex
Ms. Kate Allen
Human Resources
77 Franklin St
Boston MA 02110
617-482-1040

Boatmen's Bancshares, Inc. #109
*Boatmen's Nat'l Bank
   of St. Louis
Personnel Dept.
100 North Broadway
St. Louis MO 63102
314-425-7500

Branch Corporation #147
Branch Banking & Trust Co.
Mr. Whit Strunk
Human Resources Dept.
P.O. Box 1847
Wilson NC 27893
919-399-4291

**Brown Brothers Harriman
   & Co.
(private)
Mr. Edwin F. Stabbert
Personnel Manager
59 Wall St.
New York NY 10005
212-483-1818

California First Bank #79
Personnel Department
350 California St.
San Francisco CA 94104
415-445-0200

The Capital Group, Inc.
**Capital Guardian
  Trust Company
Mrs. Louise Weaver
Personnel Dept.
333 South Hope St.
Los Angeles CA 90071
213-486-9200

CBT Corporation #54
*Connecticut Bank and Trust Co.
Mrs. Lois Schaeneman
Mgr. of Professional Recruitment
Connecticut Bank Building
One Constitution Plaza
Hartford CT 06115
203-244-4312

Centerre Bancorporation #74
*Centerre Trust Company
  of St. Louis
Mr. Gary Klenne
Dir. of Human Resources
One Centerre Plaza
St. Louis MO 63101
314-554-6500

Central Bancorporation,
  Inc. #116
Central Trust Co.
Mrs. Sally Weinkam
Employment Manager
Human Resources Dept.
P.O. Box 1198
Cincinnati OH 45201
513-651-8534

Central Bancshares of the South,
  Inc. #119
Central Bank of Birmingham
Mr. John McNicholas
Room #902
P.O. Box 10566
Birmingham AL 35296
205-933-3781

Central Fidelity Banks, Inc. #121
Broad at Third St.
Mrs. Sherry Easter
Personnel Dept.
P.O. Box 27602
Richmond VA 23261
804-782-4000

Centran Corp. #117
Central Nat'l Bank of Cleveland
Employment Division
800 Superior Ave.
Cleveland OH 44114
216-344-5153

CharterCorp #124
First Nat'l Bank of Kansas City
Ms. Joyce Barnes
Personnel Dept.
P.O. Box 38
Kansas City MO 64183
816-221-2800

The Chase Manhattan Corp. #3
**Chase Investors
  Management Corp.
The Chase Manhattan Bank
Professional Recruitment
27th floor
One Chase Manhattan Plaza
New York NY 10081
212-552-5020

Chemical New York Corp. #6
**Chemical Bank
College Recruiting Dept.
277 Park Ave.
New York NY 10172
212-310-6746

Citicorp #1
**Citibank
Recruiting Services
153 E. 53rd St.
New York NY 10043
212-559-0978

Citizen's Fidelity Corp. #115
Citizen's Fidelity Bank & Trust
Mrs. Sharon Harris
Personnel Dept.
Citizen's Plaza
500 West Jefferson St.
Louisville KY 40296
502-581-2261

The Citizens and Southern
    Corp. #146
Ms. Zohra Holsopple
Personnel Department
P.O. Box 727
Columbia SC 29222
803-765-8234

Citizens & Southern Georgia
    Corp. #43
(acquiring Landmark Banking)
*Citizens & Southern Nat'l Bank
    of Georgia
Professional Staffing
33 North Ave.
Atlanta GA 30308
404-897-3578 (recorded message)
404-897-3023

City National Corp. #162
City National Bank
Mrs. Linda Brown
Personnel Department
120 So. Spalding Drive
Beverly Hills CA 90212
213-550-5400

Citytrust Bancorp #196
Ms. Barbara Thomas
Personnel Dept.
961 Main St.
Bridgeport, CT 06601
203-384-5212

Colonial Bankcorp, Inc. #197
Human Resources Dept.
48 Leavenworth St.
Waterbury CT 06702
203-574-7000

Colorado National Bankshares,
    Inc. #134
The Colorado Nat'l Bank
    of Denver
Human Resources Dept.
Box 5168 T.A.
Denver CO 80217
303-893-1862

Comerica, Inc. #35
*Detroit Bank and
    Trust Company
Corporate Human Resources
211 West Fort St.
Detroit MI 48226
313-222-6266

Commerce Bancshares, Inc. #83
Ms. Leslie Dermann
Personnel Dept.
P.O. Box 248
Kansas City MO 64199
816-234-2766

Commerce Union Corp. #136
Commerce Union Bank
Human Resources Dept.
One Commerce Place
Nashville TN 37219
615-749-3360

Conifer/Essex Group #161
Mr. Sylvio Demers
VP & Personnel Dir.
370 Main St.
Worcester, MA 01608
617-752-5661

Continental Bancorp, Inc. #89
Continental Bank
Mr. Joseph Ambrosino
Personnel Officer
515 Pennsylvania Ave.
Fort Washington PA 19034
215-641-8226

Continental Illinois Corp. #12
**Cont'l Ill. Nat'l Bank &
    Trust Co.
Mr. Kevin Coleman
Manager of College Relations
231 So. LaSalle St.
Chicago IL 60697
312-828-2345

Corestates Financial Corp. #34
The Philadelphia National Bank
Mrs. Alice Lovely
Human Resources Dept.
5th & Market
Philadelphia PA 19106
215-629-4556

Crocker National Corp. #15
*Crocker Investment
    Management Corp.
**Crocker National Bank
Exec. Recruitment
79 New Montgomery St.
1st floor
San Francisco CA 94105
415-983-3283

Cullen/Frost Bankers, Inc. #111
Personnel Dept.
100 W. Houston St.
San Antonio TX 78296
512-220-4011

Dauphin Deposit Corp. #155
Dauphin Deposit Bank &
    Trust Co.
Ms. Jennifer Slike
Human Resources Dept.
213 Market St.
Harrisburg PA 17101
717-255-2304

Deposit Guaranty Corp. #142
Deposit Guaranty Nat'l Bank
Personnel Dept.
P.O. Box 1200
Jackson MS 39205
601-354-8183

Dominion Bankshares Corp. #84
Dominion Bank
Mrs. Merle King
Human Resources Dept.
P.O. Box 13327
Roanoke VA 24040
703-563-7000

Equimark Corp. #141
Equibank
Ms. Carolyn Dillon
Human Resources Dept.
2 Oliver Plaza
Pittsburgh PA 15222
412-288-5896

Equitable Bancorp #113
The Equitable Trust Co.
Equitable Bank
Mr. David Clark
Personnel Dept.
Equitable Bank Center
100 South Charles St.
Baltimore MD 21201
301-547-4497

European-American
  Bancorp. #47
European-American
  Bank & Trust
Mr. Walter Kehoe
  VP Exec. Recruitment
10 Hanover Square
New York NY 10015
212-437-4102

Fidata Trust Co.
Mr. John Joyce
Mgr. of Employment
67 Broad St.
New York NY 10004
212-530-2600

Fidelcor, Inc. #63
The Fidelity Bank
Ms. Meg McNichol
Professional Recruitment Rep.
Broad & Walnut Sts.
Philadelphia PA 19109
215-985-6000

**Fiduciary Trust Co. of
  New York
(private)
Ms. Elayne Gentul
Placement Officer
Two World Trade Center
New York NY 10048
212-466-4100

Fifth Third Bancorp #149
The Fifth Third Bank
Corporate Recruiting
Personnel Dept.
38 Fountain Square Plaza
Cincinnati OH 45263
513-579-5300

First Alabama Bancshares,
  Inc. #108
Merchants Nat'l Bank of Mobile
Mr. John O'Connell
Personnel Director
P.O. Box 511
Montgomery AL 36134
205-832-8314

First of America Bank Corp. #86
First of America Bank
Mr. Kenneth Clark
VP & Personnel Director
108 E. Michigan Ave.
Kalamazoo MI 49007
616-383-9000

First American Bankshares,
  Inc. #80
First American Bank of Virginia
Mr. James Reynolds
Mgr. of Employment
1970 Chainbridge Road
McLean VA 22102
703-821-7870

First American Corp. #96
First American Bank of Nashville
Human Resources Office
First American Center
Nashville TN 37237
615-748-2084

First Atlanta Corporation #53
*The First Nat'l Bank of Atlanta
Personnel Dept.
P.O. Box 4148
N.W. Atlanta GA 30302
404-588-5000

First Bancorporation of
  Ohio #177
First National Bank of Akron
Mrs. Karen Long
Staffing Administrator
106 South Main St.
Akron OH 44308
216-384-7107

First Bank System, Inc. #14
*First Nat'l Bank of Minneapolis
Ms. Patricia Hamm
Mgr. College Recruitment
1600 First Bank Place East
Minneapolis MN 55480
612-370-5100

First Capital Corp. #183
First National Bank
Mr. Robert Spring
Personnel Department
P.O. Box 291
Jackson MS 39205
601-354-5806

First Chicago Corp. #10
*The First Nat'l Bank of Chicago
Recruitment & Development
   Services
One North State St.
5th floor
Chicago IL 60670
312-407-2446

First Citizens Corp. #166
First-Citizens Bank & Trust Co.
Mr. Mike Bailey
Personnel Dept.
P.O. Box 151
Raleigh NC 27602
919-755-7456

First City Bancorporation of
   Texas, Inc. #24
First City Nat'l Bank of Houston
College Recruiting Dept.
Human Resources Dept.
P.O. Box 2387
Houston TX 77252
713-658-7333

First Commerce Corp. #174
First Nat'l Bank of Commerce
Human Resources Dept.
P.O. Box 60279
New Orleans LA 70160
504-561-1458

First Empire State Corp. #159
Manufacturers and Traders
   Trust Co.
Mr. Thomas Hodick
Senior Recruiter
Human Resources
One M&T Plaza
Buffalo NY 14240
716-842-5157

First Florida Banks #101
First Nat'l Bank of Florida
Ms. Sarah Cardona
Personnel Dept.
P.O. Box 1810
Tampa FL 33601
813-224-1414

First Hawaiian, Inc. #126
First Hawaiian Bank
Ms. Sally Chong
Personnel Department
P.O. Box 3200
Honolulu HI 96847
808-525-7000

First Interstate Bancorp #8
First Interstate Bank
Mr. Brett Wilson
College Relations
707 Wilshire Blvd.
Los Angeles CA 90017
213-614-5901
*Also Western Asset Mgmt. Co.

First Jersey National Corp. #143
First Jersey National Bank
Mr. Paul Winberry
Personnel Dept.
One Exchange Place
Jersey City NJ 07302
201-547-7003

First Kentucky National
   Corp. #106
First Kentucky Trust Company
Ms. Daisy Hitchcock
Personnel Dept.
P.O. Box 36000
Louisville KY 40232
502-581-4200

First Maryland Bancorp #91
The First Nat'l Bank of Maryland
Ms. Mary Harrington
Personnel Dept.
25 South Charles St.
Baltimore MD 21201
301-244-4000

First Nat'l Bank of Bartlesville
Mrs. Martha Wallen
Personnel Department
P.O. Box 999
Bartlesville OK 74005
918-337-3000

First Natl'l Bank & Trust Co.
Mr. Gerald Dimon
Personnel Director
P.O. Box 81008
Lincoln NE 68501
402-471-1448

First National Cincinnati
   Corp. #125
First Nat'l Bank, Cincinnati
Miss Kathy Beechem
Dir. of Emp. and Recruitment
425 Walnut St.
Cincinnati OH 45202
513-632-4000

First Nat'l State Bancorp. #32
First Fidelity Bank
First Nat'l State Bank
   of New Jersey
Human Resources Department
500 Broad St.
Newark NJ 07192
201-565-3200

First Oklahoma Bancorporation,
   Inc. #131
*The First Nat'l Bank & Trust
   Co. of Oklahoma City
Mr. Thomas Govan
Personnel Department
P.O. Box 25189
Oklahoma City OK 73125
405-272-4000

First Pennsylvania Corp. #73
*First Pennsylvania Bank
Ms. Karen Kirchner
Human Resources
   Department
1500 Market St. 14th floor
Philadelphia PA 19101
215-786-5000

First Railroad & Banking
   Company of Georgia #127
Georgia Railroad Bank &
   Trust Co.
Ms. Yvonne Holland
P.O. Box 2162
Augusta GA 30913
404-823-2753

First Security Corporation #77
Mr. Robert Dove
Personnel Department
P.O. Box 30004
Salt Lake City UT 84130
801-350-5311

First Tennessee Nat'l Corp. #82
Ms. Pat Brown
Employment Services
P.O. Box 84
Memphis TN 38101
901-523-5308
Also First Tenn. Inv. Mgmt., Inc.

*First Trust Company of
   Saint Paul
Ms. Cindi Iacarella
Human Resources
332 Minnesota St.
St. Paul MN 55101
612-291-5653

First Union Corp. #49
*First Union Nat'l Bank
Ms. Shannon McFayden
Personnel Department
   PERS-4
1100 First Union Plaza
Charlotte NC 28288
704-374-6565

First Virginia Banks, Inc. #135
First Virginia Bank
Mr. Guy G. Harper III
Personnel Department
One First Virginia Plaza
6400 Arlington Blvd.
Falls Church VA 22046
703-241-3137

First Wisconsin Corp. #70
First Wisconsin Trust Co.
Ms. Mary Lukas
Employment Manager
777 East Wisconsin Ave.
Milwaukee WI 53202
414-765-4151

Fleet Financial Group, Inc. #67
Fleet Nat'l Bank
Mr. Richard J. Marshall
College Recruiting Coordinator
Personnel Department
111 Westminster St.
Providence RI 02903
401-278-6282

Florida Nat'l Banks of Florida,
   Inc. #72
Florida National Bank
Human Resource Mgmt. Division
P.O. Box 689
Jacksonville FL 32201
904-359-5088

Fuji Bank & Trust Co. #145
(cont. by The Fuji Bank, Ltd.)
Administration Department
One World Trade Center
Suite 8067
New York NY 10048
212-839-6800

General Bancshares Corp. #173
General Bank
Mrs. Judy Robbins
Human Resources Department
901 Washington St.
St. Louis MO 63101
314-982-4287

Harris Bancorp, Inc.
(sub. of Bank of Montreal)
**Harris Trust and Savings Bank
Mr. Von Ponder
Human Resources Dept.
111 West Monroe St.
Chicago IL 60690
312-461-2121

Hartford National Corp. #60
First Bank (New Haven CT)
*Hartford Nat'l Bank & Trust Co.
Human Resources Department
777 Main St.
Hartford CT 06115
203-728-2000

Hawkeye Bancorporation #180
Mr. Donald Runger
Senior Vice President
600 Stephens Building
7th & Locust St.
Des Moines IA 50307
515-284-1930

Heritage Bancorporation #171
Heritage Bank
Ms. Maria Sannino
Route 70 & Cuthbert Blvd.
Cherry Hill NJ 08002
609-662-2700

Hibernia Corp. #188
*Hibernia Nat'l Bank in
    New Orleans
Recruiting
P.O. Box 61540
New Orleans LA 70161
504-586-5518

Horizon Bancorp #137
Horizon Bank
Mr. Greg Pogue
Personnel Department
334 Madison Ave.
Morristown NJ 07960
201-285-2103

Huntington Bancshares, Inc. #69
The Huntington Nat'l Bank
Employment Office
HCO421
41 S. High St.
Columbus OH 43215
614-476-8300

Indiana National Corp. #112
*Indiana National Bank
Ms. Leslie Lange
Professional Recruiter
Five Indiana Square
Indianapolis IN 46266
317-266-6767

Industrial Bank of Japan #160
Administration Dept.
245 Park Ave. 21st Fl.
New York NY 10167
212-557-3500

InterFirst Corp. #18
*InterFirst Bank Dallas
Human Resources Department
P.O. Box 83000
Dallas TX 75283-0119
214-977-2610

Irving Bank Corporation #23
*Irving Trust Company
Ms. Kim Healey
College Relations Center
One Wall St.
New York NY 10005
212-635-1111

Israel Discount Bank of
    New York #103
Human Resources Department
511 Fifth Ave.
New York NY 10017
212-551-8664

IVB Financial #178
Industrial Valley Bank
Personnel Department
1700 Market St.
Philadelphia PA 19103
215-576-3500

Key Banks Inc. #68
Key Trust Company
Key Bank
Ms. Patricia Smaldone
Human Resources Department
60 State St.
Albany NY 12207
518-447-3245

Landmark Banking Corp.
   of Florida #100
(acq. by Citizens & Southern
   Georgia Corp.)
Landmark First Nat'l Bank
   of Fort Lauderdale
Ms. Susan Johnson
Personnel Manager
P.O. Box 5367
Fort Lauderdale FL 33310
305-765-2000

LaSalle National Bank #198
Mrs. Kathryn West
Human Resources Dept.
135 So. LaSalle St.
Chicago IL 60690
312-443-2000

Liberty United Bancorp,
   Inc. #193
United Kentucky Bank
Liberty Nat'l Bank & Trust Co.
Mr. Paul Corrington
Management Development
One Riverfront Plaza
Louisville KY 40202
502-566-2000

Lincoln First Banks Inc. #81
Lincoln First Bank
Personnel Department
One Lincoln First Square
Rochester NY 14643
716-258-5000

Lloyds Bank California #130
(cont. by Lloyds Bank Ltd.)
Mr. James Haywood
612 So. Flower St.
Los Angeles CA 90017
213-613-3811

Manufacturers Hanover
   Corp. #4
**Manufacturers Hanover
   Trust Corp.
College Recruiting
Grand Central Station
P.O. Box 3732
New York NY 10163
212-644-7782

Manufacturers National
   Corp. #59
*Manufacturers Nat'l Bank
   of Detroit
Ms. Libby Graham
Personnel Department
411 W. Lafayette
Detroit MI 48226
313-222-4610

Marine Corp. #132
The Marine Trust Co.
Marine Bank
Mr. Jeffery Struve
Personnel Department
P.O. Box 2071
Milwaukee WI 53201
414-765-3000

Marine Midland Banks, Inc. #17
Marine Midland Bank
Ms. Jan Ahlstrom
College Relations
140 Broadway 9th floor
New York NY 10015
212-440-1884

Marshall & Ilsley
   Corp. #97
M & I Inv. Mgmt. Corp.
M & I Marshall &
   Ilsley Bank
Mr. Thomas Deisinger
Employment Representative
770 North Water St.
Milwaukee WI 53202
414-765-8365

Maryland National
   Corp. #50
Maryland National Bank
Mrs. Cynthia V. Hunt
Manager of Trainee Staffing
   and Development
225 North Calvert
Baltimore MD 21202
301-244-5348

MCorp #22
Mercantile Securities Corp.
Write to MCorp
Ms. Lynn Miterko
P.O. Box 2629
Houston TX 77252
713-236-7616
College Relations
P.O. Box 225415
Dallas TX 75265
214-698-6000

Mellon National Corp #11
*Girard Bank
**Mellon Bank
Ms. Barbara Hudson
Mgr. of College Relations
   & Recruiting
One Mellon Bank Center
Room 1830
Pittsburgh PA 15258
412-234-5315

Mercantile Bancorporation
   Inc. #64
*Mercantile Trust Co. of St. Louis
Mr. Arno Ellis
Human Resources Department
P.O. Box 524
St. Louis MO 63166
314-425-2525

Mercantile Bankshares
   Corp. #156
*Mercantile-Safe Deposit
   & Trust Co.
Ms. Cynthia Rallo
766 Old Hammond Ferry Road
Linthicum MD 21090
301-347-8051

Merchants National Corp. #150
Merchants National Bank
Human Resources
One Merchants Plaza Suite 808
Indianapolis IN 46255
317-267-7554

Meridian Bancorp, Inc. #71
American Bank & Trust Co.
   of Pennsylvania
Mr. Robert Palko
Human Resources Department
P.O. Box 1102
Reading PA 19603
215-320-2411

Michigan National Corp. #56
Michigan National Bank
Professional Staffing Dept.
29777 Telegraph Rd.
Onyx Plaza Suite 2201
Southfield MI 48034
313-354-8195

Midlantic Banks Inc. #52
Midlantic National Bank
Mr. Gilbert Sager
Human Resources Department
P.O. Box 600
Edison NJ 08818
201-321-8560

Midwest Financial Group #164
Commercial National Bank
Personnel Department
301 S.W. Adams
Peoria IL 61631
309-655-5332

Mitsui Mfg. Bank #185
Ms. Garnet Hyder
Personnel Dept. 4th Fl.
515 So. Figueroa
Los Angeles CA 90071
213-485-0331

Moore Financial Group, Inc. #120
Idaho First Nat'l Bank
Employment Services
P.O. Box 50
Boise ID 83728
208-384-7516

J.P. Morgan & Co. Inc. #5
**Morgan Guaranty
   Trust Company
Ms. Patricia Simboli
Corporate Recruiting Department
23 Wall St.
New York NY 10015
212-208-4617

Multibank Financial Corp. #186
South Shore Bank
Mr. Frank Belcastro
Personnel Department
1400 Hancock St.
Quincy MA 02169
617-847-3201

Nat'l Bancshares Corp.
   of Texas #139
Nat'l Bank of Commerce
Human Resources Department
P.O. Box 121
San Antonio TX 78291
512-225-2511 (9 to 3)

National Bank of Alaska
Personnel Department
P.O. Box 600
Anchorage AK 99510
907-276-1132

National Bank of Washington
Ms. Karen Fizer
Human Resources Department
4340 Conn. Ave. NW
Washington DC 20008
202-537-2027

National City Corp. #31
*National City Bank
Mr. Timothy McFarland
Personnel Department
National City Center
1900 East 9th St.
Cleveland OH 44114
216-575-2468
BancOhio Nat'l Bank
Mrs. Zuni Corkerton
Human Resources
155 East Broad St.
Columbus OH 43265
614-463-8180

National Community Bank of
   New Jersey #191
Ms. Eleanor Baumann
Personnel Department
15 Ames Avenue
Rutherford NJ 07070
201-845-1614

National Westminster Bank
  USA #40
(owned by Nat'l Westminster
  Bank PLC London)
Ms. Cynthia Gardner
Human Resources Department
175 Water St.
New York NY 10038
212-602-1645

NBD Bancorp, Inc. #28
**Nat'l Bank of Detroit
Professional Employment Dept.
611 Woodward Ave.
Detroit MI 48226
313-225-1681

NCNB Corporation #25
*North Carolina Nat'l Bank
Mr. Craig Buffie
Corporate Personnel Department
One NCNB Plaza
Charlotte NC 28255
704-374-8235

New Jersey National Corp. #190
New Jersey National Bank
Employment Office CN5
Pennington NJ 08534
609-771-5700

Norstar Bancorp Inc. #45
Mr. Joseph Pelgrin
1450 Western Ave.
Albany NY 12203
518-447-4043

Northeast Bancorp, Inc. #176
Union Trust Co.
Ms. Marilyn Goodwin
Personnel Officer
P.O. Box 404
New Haven CT 06502
203-773-5647

Northern Trust Corp. #51
*Northern Trust Company
Human Resources Department
50 South LaSalle St.
Chicago IL 60675
312-630-6000

Norwest Corp. #20
*Norwest Bank Minneapolis
Mrs. Helen Getzkin
Human Resources Department
8th St. & Marquette Ave.
Minneapolis MN 55479
612-372-0430

The Ohio Citizens
  Trust Company
Employment Manager
Employee Relations
P.O. Box 1688
Toledo OH 43603
419-259-6710

Old Kent Financial Corp. #95
Old Kent Bank & Trust Co.
Mr. Kevin Cabat
Personnel Department
One Vandenburg Center
Grand Rapids MI 49503
616-774-5298

Old Stone Corp. #140
Old Stone Bank
Mr. Joel Cohn
Personnel Department
180 South Main St.
Providence RI 02903
401-278-2206

Omaha Nat'l Corp. #158
Omaha Nat'l Bank
Ms. Nancy O'Brien
Personnel Department
1700 Farnam St.
Omaha NE 68102
402-348-6401

ONB Corporation #187
(Old Nat'l Bancorporation)
Mr. Alfonso Marsh
Employment Officer
West 428 Riverside
Spokane WA 99201
509-456-2188

Orbanco Financial Services
   Corp. #199
The Oregon Bank
Mr. Sydney T. Brown
VP Personnel
P.O. Box 3066
Portland OR 97208
503-222-7560

Pan American Banks, Inc. #192
Personnel Department
250 Southeast First St.
Miami FL 33131
305-577-5700

Peoples Bancorporation #165
Peoples Nat'l Bank
Employment
P.O. Box 720
Seattle WA 98111
206-344-3616

PNC Financial Corp. #27
Provident Nat'l Bank
*Pittsburgh Nat'l Bank
Mr. William Lenaghen
Personnel Department
Fifth Avenue & Wood St.
Pittsburgh PA 15265
412-355-2650

Rainier Bancorporation #46
Rainier National Bank
Recruiting Services
P.O. Box 3966
Seattle WA 98124
206-621-5965

RepublicBank Corp. #19
**RepublicBank Dallas
University Relations
P.O. Box 225961
Dallas TX 75265
214-922-5449

Republic New York Corp. #30
Republic Nat'l Bank of New York
Human Resources Department
452 Fifth Ave.
New York NY 10018
212-930-6000

Riggs National Corp. #76
Riggs National Bank
Employment Office
1120 Vermont Ave. N.W.
Washington DC 20005
202-835-6423

RIHT Financial Corp. #157
Hospital Trust Investors
Rhode Island Hospital Trust
   National Bank
Human Resources Department
One Hospital Trust Plaza
Providence RI 02903
401-278-8300

Schroders Inc. #170
J. Henry Schroder Bank & Trust
Miss Joan Field
Personnel Department
One State St.
New York NY 10004
212-269-6500

Seafirst Corp.
(Sub. of BankAmerica Corp.)
Seattle-First Nat'l Bank
Ms. Gloria Thurlow
Sr. Recruiting Officer
P.O. Box 3977
Seattle WA 98124
206-583-4795

Security Bancorp #200
Mr. George Kinlen
Personnel Department
16333 Trenton Rd.
Southgate MI 48195
313-281-5000

Security Pacific Corp. #7
*Security Pacific Investment
    Managers, Inc.
Security Pacific Bank
Personnel Dept. H18-2
P.O. Box 2097
Terminal Annex
Los Angeles CA 90051
213-613-6284

Shawmut Corp. #58
The Shawmut Bank
Mrs. Vicki Smith
College Relations
One Federal St.
Boston MA 02211
617-292-2319

Society Corp. #66
Society National Bank
Mr. Joe Covey
Employee Relations
127 Public Square
Cleveland OH 44114
216-622-8255

South Carolina Nat'l
    Corp. #93
South Carolina Nat'l Bank
Mr. John Hamilton
Mgr. of Career Development
Greystone Boulevard
Columbia SC 29202
803-765-4457

Southeast Banking Corp. #33
Southeast Bank
Mrs. Sharon Baro
Corporate Recruitment 5th floor
200 South Biscayne Boulevard
Miami FL 33131
305-375-6060

SouthTrust Corp. #110
SouthTrust Bank of Alabama
Personnel Department
P.O. Box 2554
Birmingham AL 35290
205-254-5393

Sovran Financial Corp. #42
Sovran Bank
Mr. John Payne
Personnel Department
P.O. Box 27025
Richmond VA 23261
804-788-2524

Springfield Marine Bank
Ms. Becky Hendricks
Personnel Department
East Old State Capitol Plaza
Springfield IL 62701
217-525-9755

State Street Boston Corp. #81
*State Street Bank & Trust Co.
Ms. Sally Sands
Personnel Office
P.O. Box 351
Boston MA 02101
617-654-3371

Suburban Bancorp #123
Suburban Bank
Management Recruitment
6610 Rockledge Drive
Bethesda MD 20814
301-270-5000

Sumitomo Bank of
  California #129
Ms. Iris Cox
Personnel Dept. 8th floor
320 California St.
San Francisco CA 94104
415-445-8009

Summit Bancorp #195
Summit Trust Company
Mr. William J. Beyer
Sr. VP Human Resources
100 Industrial Road
Berkeley Hts NJ 07922
201-522-8400

Sun Banks, Inc. #37
Sun Bank
Ms. Michelle Linnert
27 West Church Street
Orlando FL 32801
305-237-4314

Sunwest Financial Services,
  Inc. #167
Sunwest Bank of Albuquerque
Ms. Sharon Wright
Human Resources Department
P.O. Box 25500
Albuquerque NM 87125
505-765-3001

Texas American Bancshares
  Inc. #62
Texas American Bank
Mr. Whit Smith
Dir. of Recruiting
  & Placement
P.O. Box 2050
Fort Worth TX 76113
817-338-8196

Texas Commerce Bancshares,
  Inc. #21
*Texas Commerce Bank
Employment Division
P.O. Box 2558
Houston TX 77252
713-236-4285

Third National Corp. #87
Third National Bank in Nashville
Mrs. Lynn Goodman
Human Resources Department
201 4th Ave. No.
Nashville TN 37244
615-748-4096

Toledo Trustcorp, Inc. #154
The Toledo Trust Company
Employee Relations Dept.
Three Seagate
Toledo OH 43603
419-259-8100

Trust Company of Georgia #61
(merged with Sun Banks)
*Trust Company Bank
Mr. John Semler
Personnel Department
P.O. Box 4418
Atlanta GA 30302
404-588-7060

Union Bank #44
Exec. Recruitment Office
445 South Figueroa St.
Los Angeles CA 90071
213-236-5500

Union National Corp. #151
The Union National Bank
Mr. Edward Sullivan
Human Resources Dept.
P.O. Box 837
Pittsburgh PA 15230
412-644-8484

Union Planters Corp. #179
Union Planters Nat'l Bank
Employment Department
67 Madison Ave.
Memphis TN 38103
901-523-6664

Union Trust Bancorp #168
Union Trust Co.
  of Maryland
Mr. Vincent DalFonzo
Personnel Department
P.O. Box 1077
Baltimore MD 21203
301-332-5087

United Bancorp of
  Arizona #189
Human Resources Dept.
P.O. Box 2908
Phoenix AZ 85012-2908
602-248-2146

United Banks of Colorado,
  Inc. #88
United Capital Management
United Bank of Colorado
Ms. Jean Marshall
Personnel Manager
One United Bank Center
1700 Lincoln St. Suite 3200
Denver CO 80274
303-861-4700

United Jersey Banks #94
United Jersey Bank
Ms. Susan Schranz
Personnel Department
P.O. Box 2066
Princeton NJ 08540
609-987-3200

United Missouri Bancshares,
  Inc. #122
United Missouri Investment
  Counseling Service
United Missouri Bank of
  Kansas City
Mr. Ray Fuller
Personnel Department
P.O. Box 226
Kansas City MO 64141
816-556-7960

United Virginia Bankshares
  Inc. #65
Capitoline Investment Services
United Virginia Bank
Ms. Brenda Watts
Personnel Department
P.O. Box 26665
Richmond VA 23261
804-782-5000

U.S. Bancorp #48
United States Nat'l Bank
  of Oregon
Ms. Angela Burns
Personnel Department
P.O. Box 8837
Portland OR 97208
503-225-6163

U.S. Trust Corp. #153
*United States Trust Company
  of New York
Ms. Sharon Simmons
Personnel Department
45 Wall St. 18th floor
New York NY 10005
212-806-4709

Valley National Corp. #39
Valley Nat'l Bank of Arizona
Career Services
P.O. Box 71
Phoenix AZ 85001
602-261-1093

The Wachovia Corp. #41
*Wachovia Bank and Trust Co.
Mrs. Karen Gilbert
Personnel Department
301 North Main St.
Winston-Salem NC 27102
919-770-5000

Wells Fargo & Company #13
**Wells Fargo Investment
   Advisors
Wells Fargo Bank
Placement Services 15th floor
475 Sansome St.
San Francisco CA 94163
415-396-2767

Whitney Holding Corp. #163
Whitney National Bank
Ms. Anne Leach
VP Personnel
228 St. Charles Ave.
New Orleans LA 70161
504-586-7418

*Wilmington Trust
   Company #169
Mr. William Young
Personnel Department
Rodney Square North
Wilmington DE 19890
302-651-1000

Worthen Banking #152
Worthen Bank & Trust
Human Resources Dept.
P.O. Box 1681
Little Rock AR 72203
501-378-1000

Zions Utah Bancorporation #133
Zions First National Bank
Mrs. Earleen Gregory
Personnel Department
350 Kennecott Building
P.O. Box 2277
Salt Lake City UT 84133
801-524-4690

Investment Banking and Brokerage Firms

These companies are listed in alphabetical order. Unless otherwise noted, references given are for positions in investment banking rather than other management training programs. Those seeking a career as a securities broker should contact individual branch offices, as explained in Chapter 8.

Alex. Brown & Sons
(public)
Personnel Department
135 E. Baltimore St.
Baltimore MD 21203
301-727-1700

Bateman, Eichler, Hill
 Richards Inc.
(private)
Ms. Sharon Yee
Human Resources Department
700 South Flower St.
Los Angeles CA 90017
213-625-3545

Bear, Stearns & Co. Inc.
(public)
Ms. Ann Corwin
Personnel Department
5 Hanover Square 8th floor
New York NY 10004
212-952-5000

Cowen & Co.
(private)
Mr. Stuart Goodman
Controller
One Battery Park Plaza
New York NY 10004
212-460-0700

Dain Bosworth Inc.
Ms. Margaret Molde
Human Resources Department
100 Dain Tower
Minneapolis MN 55402
612-371-2948

Dillon, Read & Co. Inc.
(private)
Ms. Lori Hinchman
Personnel Department
535 Madison Ave.
New York NY 10022
212-906-7000

Donaldson, Lufkin &
 Jenrette Securities Corporation
(Sub. of Equitable Life)
Ms. Jeanne Ruscio
Human Resources
140 Broadway
New York NY 10005
212-504-3000

Drexel Burnham Lambert Inc.
(private)
Personnel Dept. 24th floor
60 Broad St.
New York NY 10004
212-480-6000

A. G. Edwards & Sons, Inc.
(public)
Ms. Nancy Gough
Employment Manager
One North Jefferson
St. Louis MO 63103
314-289-3000

The First Boston Corporation
(private)
Ms. Kate Higgins
Corporate Finance Department
Park Ave. Plaza
New York NY 10055
212-909-2000

Goldman, Sachs
  & Co.
(private)
Personnel Department
85 Broad St.
New York NY 10004
212-902-1000

Gruntal Financial Corp.
(public)
Ms. Lee Hirsch
Personnel Director
14 Wall St.
New York NY 10005
212-267-8800

Hambrecht & Quist Inc.
(private)
Ms. Jena Brandeberry
Dir. of Personnel
235 Montgomery St.
5th floor
San Francisco CA 94104
415-986-5500

Herzfeld & Stern Inc.
(private)
Ms. Karen Borschel
Human Resources
  Department
30 Broad St.
New York NY 10004
212-480-1800

E.F. Hutton &
  Company Inc.
(public)
Ms. Yvette Bowden
University Relations
One Battery Park Plaza
New York NY 10004
212-742-5000

Kidder, Peabody & Co., Inc.
(private)
for investment banking:
Mr. Joseph Labita
Employment Mgr.
for Management Training
  Program:
Ms. Patricia May
Personnel Department
Two Broadway
New York NY 10004
212-510-3000

Ladenburg, Thalman & Co. Inc.
(private)
Ms. Carla Gurji
Personnel Department
540 Madison Ave.
New York NY 10022
212-940-0100

Lazard Freres & Co.
(private)
(NYC, London, Paris)
Ms. Lenore Cicchese
Mgr. of Personnel
One Rockefeller Plaza
New York NY 10020
212-489-6600

Merrill Lynch & Co., Inc.
(public)
for investment banking:
Ms. Elizabeth Keating
Merrill Lynch Capital Markets
  for Corporate Intern or other
  management training
  programs:
Ms. Kathy Seichs
College Relations
One Liberty Plaza
165 Broadway
New York NY 10008
212-637-7455

Montgomery Securities
(private)
Ms. Patricia Franze
Personnel Department
600 Montgomery St.
San Francisco CA 94111
415-627-2000

Morgan Stanley & Co., Inc.
(public)
Mrs. Patricia Palumbo
Recruitment Coordinator for
    Investment Banking
1251 Avenue of the Americas
New York NY 10020
212-974-4000

Oppenheimer & Co., Inc.
(private)
Mr. Gerard Conlon
Personnel Department 17th floor
110 Wall Street
New York NY 10005
212-825-4000

Paine Webber Group, Inc.
(public)
Human Resources Department
120 Broadway 8th floor
New York NY 10271
212-437-2121

Piper, Jaffray & Hopwood Inc.
(public)
Mrs. Angela Eastburn
Human Resources Department
P.O. Box 28
Minneapolis MN 55440
612-342-6000

Prudential-Bache Securities
(private)
Employment Department
100 Gold St.
New York NY 10292
212-791-1000

Robertson, Colman & Stephens
(private)
Mr. John Sanders
Personnel Department
One Embarcadero Center
San Francisco CA 94111
415-781-9700

Robinson Humphrey/
    American Express Inc.
(sub. of American Express)
Miss Karen Rollo
Director of Personnel
3333 Peachtree Road N.E.
    7th floor
Atlanta GA 30326
404-266-6000

Rotan Mosle Inc.
(private)
Ms. Krystyna Jeffries
Personnel Dept. 38th floor
700 Louisiana
Houston TX 77002
713-236-3000

L.F. Rothschild, Unterberg,
    Towbin, Inc.
(public)
Personnel Dept. 45th floor
55 Water St.
New York NY 10041
212-412-1000

Salomon Brothers Inc.
(div. of Phibro-Salomon)
(public)
Ms. Christine Simpson
Corporate Finance
One New York Plaza
New York NY 10004
212-747-7000

Shearson Lehman Brothers Inc.,
   an American Express Company
Employment
125 Broad St. 8th floor
New York NY 10004
212-323-7401

Smith Barney, Harris Upham &
   Co., Inc.
(private)
Mr. Toby Wesson
Corporate Finance Department
1345 Avenue of Americas
New York NY 10105
212-603-8800

Thomson McKinnon
   Securities Inc.
(private)
Mrs. Pat Kiley
Human Resources Department
One New York Plaza
New York NY 10004
212-482-6410

Tucker Anthony & R. L. Day
(div. of John Hancock
   Mutual Life)
Ms. Connie Gonzalez
Personnel Department
120 Broadway
New York NY 10271
212-618-7400

Wertheim & Co., Inc.
(private)
Ms. Veronica Kotowicz
Personnel Department
200 Park Ave.
New York NY 10166
212-578-0200

Dean Witter Reynolds, Inc.
(div. of Sears)
Ms. Kathy Brent
Personnel Department
5 World Trade Center 8th floor
New York NY 10048
212-524-2222

B. C. Ziegler & Co.
(public - sub. of Ziegler Co.)
Mr. Neil L. Fuerbringer
VP—Administration
215 North Main St.
West Bend WI 53095
414-334-5521

Investment Counselors and Mutual Funds

The firms listed below are the largest in their industries. To obtain specific numbers on the amount of assets they manage, consult the *Money Market Directory* and Wiesenberger's *Investment Companies* (see "Resources").

Not all of these firms hire B.A.'s as Research Analysts or Assistants. It is best to contact each firm in which you have a potential interest, ask to speak with the Director of Personnel, and ask what particular credentials they are seeking.

Look also under "Banks" for listings of investment advisors that are bank subsidiaries, such as Capitoline Investment Services (a subsidiary of United Virginia Bankshares).

Fred Alger Management Co., Inc.
75 Maiden Lane
New York NY 10038
212-806-8800

Alliance Capital
  Management Corp.
(owned by Donaldson, Lufkin
  & Jenrette)
140 Broadway
New York NY 10005
212-902-4000
115 South LaSalle St.
Chicago IL 60603
312-368-0066
3600 Piper Jaffray Tower
Minneapolis MN 55402
612-332-1544
Bank of America Center
  Suite 4600
555 California St.
San Francisco CA 94104
415-434-4405

Analytic Investment Management
2222 Martin St. Suite 230
Irvine CA 92715
714-833-0294

Atalanta Sosnoff Capital Corp.
499 Park Ave.
New York NY 10022
212-755-2800

Atlanta Capital Management Co.
230 Peachtree St. N.W.
Suite 2200
Atlanta GA 30303-1544
404-688-4405

David L. Babson & Co., Inc.
One Boston Place
Boston MA 02108
617-723-7540

Batterymarch Financial
  Management
600 Atlantic Ave.
Boston MA 02210
617-973-9300

BEA Associates, Inc.
One Citicorp Center, 58th floor
153 East 53rd St.
New York NY 10022
212-832-2626

Bernstein-Macaulay, Inc.
(sub. of Shearson Lehman
  Brothers Inc.)
410 Park Ave.
New York NY 10022
212-826-1500

Beutel Goodman Capital
  Mgmt. Ltd.
2030 Texas Commerce Tower
Houston TX 77002
713-221-1790

George D. Bjurman & Associates
10100 Santa Monica Boulevard
Suite 2300
Los Angeles CA 90067
213-553-6577

The Boston Company, Inc.
(parent of The Boston Company
  Institutional Investors, Inc.)
(sub. of Shearson Lehman/
  American Express Inc.)
One Boston Place
Boston MA 02106
617-722-7000
241 South Figueroa St.
Suite 340
Los Angeles CA 90012
213-625-7941

John W. Bristol & Co., Inc.
233 Broadway 41st floor
New York NY 10007
212-267-9000

Brundage, Story & Rose
One Broadway
New York NY 10004
212-269-3050

Campbell Advisors, Inc.
342 Madison Ave.
New York NY 10173
212-687-6960

Capital Consultants, Inc.
2300 Southwest First
Portland OR 97201
503-241-1200

Capital Research & Management
333 South Hope St.
Los Angeles CA 90071
213-486-9200

Capital Supervisors, Inc.
20 North Clark St.
Chicago IL 60602
312-236-8271

Century Capital Associates
767 Third Ave.
New York NY 10017
212-909-5800

Chicago Title and Trust
  Company
111 West Washington St.
Chicago IL 60602
312-630-2000

CIGNA Investment Mgmt.
  Company
Hartford CT 06152
203-726-6000

CMB Investment Counselors
1880 Century Park East Suite 600
Los Angeles CA 90067
213-557-1500

Cole, Yeager & Wood, Inc.
630 Fifth Ave.
New York NY 10111
212-765-5350

Colonial Mgmt. Associates, Inc.
(sub. of State Mutual Life)
75 Federal St.
Boston MA 02110
617-426-3750

Columbia Management Co.
1301 Southwest Fifth
Portland OR 97201
503-222-3600

The Common Fund
P.O. Box 940
Fairfield CT 06430
203-254-1211

Cooke & Bieler, Inc.
1435 Walnut St.
Philadelphia PA 19102
215-567-1101

Degnan and Gillespie
    Fixed-Income Management
45 North Broad St.
Ridgewood NJ 07450
201-445-4970

Delaware Investment Advisers
(investment counseling)
Delaware Mgmt. Company, Inc.
(mutual fund)
#10 Penn Center Plaza
Philadelphia PA 19103
215-568-5880

Discount Corp. of New York
    Advisors
58 Pine St.
New York NY 10005
212-248-8989

Dodge & Cox, Inc.
One Post St.
San Francisco CA 94104
415-981-1710

Drexel Burnham Lambert
    Investment Advisors
3 Mellon Bank Center
15th St. & So. Penn Sq.
Philadelphia PA 19102
215-561-8060

Dreyfus Corporation
(mutual fund)
767 Fifth Ave.
New York NY 10022
212-715-6000
Dreyfus Management Inc.
(investment counseling)
212-715-6454

Eagle Management & Trust
    Company
1200 River Oaks Bank Tower
Houston TX 77019
713-526-8401

Eaton & Howard, Vance
    Sanders Inc.
24 Federal St.
Boston MA 02110
617-482-8260

Eberstadt Asset
    Management, Inc.
(investment counseling)
Eberstadt Fund
    Management, Inc.
(mutual fund)
(sub. of Alliance Capital Mgmt.
    Corp.)

Endowment Mgmt. &
    Research Corp.
(owned by Baring Brothers,
    London)
77 Franklin St.
Boston MA 02110
617-357-8480

Essex Investment Mgmt.
    Co., Inc.
Ten Post Office Square Suite 1330
Boston MA 02109
617-482-4870

Fayez Sarofim & Company
Two Houston Center Suite 2907
Houston TX 77010
713-654-4484

Fidelity Group of Mutual Funds
Fidelity Management
82 Devonshire St.
Boston MA 02109
617-479-6200

First Manhattan Co.
437 Madison Ave.
New York NY 10022
212-832-4400

First Pacific Advisors, Inc.
10301 West Pico Blvd.
Los Angeles CA 90064
213-277-4900

Fischer, Francis, Trees, & Watts
717 Fifth Ave., 14th floor
New York NY 10022
212-350-8050

FJW Financial Management, Inc.
1001 Southwest Fifth 1919
Portland OR 97204
503-226-1444

Forstman-Leff Associates
55 E. 52nd St.
New York NY 10055
212-644-9888

Fort Hill Investors Mgmt. Corp.
260 Franklin St.
Boston MA 02110
617-439-4488

Funds Advisory Company
(investment counseling)
Funds, Inc.
(mutual fund)
(sub. of Criterion Mgmt. Co.)
333 Clay St. Suite 4300
Houston TX 77002
713-751-2400

Gardner and Preston Moss, Inc.
One Winthrop Square
Boston MA 02110
617-482-6500

General American Investors
   Co. Inc.
330 Madison Ave.
New York NY 10017
212-916-8400

General Electric Investment Co.
292 Long Ridge Road
P.O. Box 7900
Stamford CT 06904
203-357-4100

Glickenhaus & Company
6 East 43rd St.
New York NY 10017
212-953-7800

David G. Greene & Company
30 Wall Street
New York NY 10005
212-344-5180

G. T. Capital Management, Inc.
601 Montgomery St.
San Francisco CA 94111
415-392-6181

Hoisington Investment
   Mgmt. Co.
333 Clay St. Suite 4440
Houston TX 77002
713-650-1004

IDS Advisory Group
(investment counseling)
3100 IDS Tower
Minneapolis MN 55402
612-372-3335

Investors Diversified
  Services, Inc.
(mutual fund)
3000 IDS Tower
612-372-3131

Institutional Capital Corporation
230 West Monroe St. Suite 2930
Chicago IL 60606
312-641-7200

INVESCO Capital
  Management, Inc.
100 Colony Square
Suite 1400
1175 Peachtree St. N.E.
Atlanta GA 30361
404-892-0896
(also Miami FL)

Investment Advisers, Inc.
P.O. Box 1160
Minneapolis MN 55440
612-371-7780
(also Houston TX)

Investment & Capital
  Mgmt. Corp.
Two Continental Towers
1701 Golf Road
Rolling Meadows IL 60008
312-439-8500

The Investment Counsel
  Company
56 E. Pine St. Suite 200
Orlando FL 32801
305-841-6241

Jamison, Eaton & Wood, Inc.
39 Main St.
Chatham NJ 07928
201-635-6700

Jennison Associates Capital
  Corp.
466 Lexington Ave.
New York NY 10017
212-421-1000

Kemper Financial Services Inc.
120 S. LaSalle St.
Chicago IL 60603
312-845-1958

Kennedy Associates, Inc.
Financial Center Bldg.
Suite 2400
Seattle WA 98161
206-624-9640

Keystone Massachusetts Group
99 High St.
Boston MA 02110
617-338-3200

Lazard Freres & Co.
One Rockefeller Plaza
New York NY 10020
212-489-6600

Lehman Management Co., Inc.
(sub. of Shearson Lehman/
  American Express Inc.)
55 Water St.
New York NY 10041
212-558-1500

Lincoln Capital Management Co.
200 South Wacker Drive
Suite 2100
Chicago IL 60606
312-559-2880

Loomis, Sayles & Co., Inc.
(owned by New England Mutual
   Life)
One Financial Center
Boston MA 02111
617-482-2450
Three First Nat'l Plaza
Chicago IL 60603
312-346-9750
150 E. 52nd St.
New York NY 10022
212-644-1120

Lord, Abbett & Co.
63 Wall St.
New York NY 10005
212-425-8720

MacKay-Shields Financial Corp.
551 Fifth Ave.
New York NY 10176
212-986-1100

Massachusetts Financial Services
(owned by Sun Life of Canada)
200 Berkeley St.
Boston MA 02116
617-423-3500

Mathers & Company, Inc.
125 South Wacker Drive
Chicago IL 60606
312-236-8215

McCowan Associates Inc.
70 Pine St. 35th floor
New York NY 10270
212-480-8700

McGlinn Capital
   Management, Inc.
P.O. Box 6158
Wyomissing PA 19610
215-374-5125

C.S. McKee & Company
2900 U.S. Steel Building
Pittsburgh PA 15219
412-566-1234

Merrill Lynch Asset Management
(sub. of Merrill Lynch & Co.)
800 Scudder's Mill Road
Plainsboro NJ 08536
609-282-2000

MH Investment Counsel
445 South Figueroa St.
Los Angeles CA 90071
213-612-3660
1430 E. Missouri Ave.
Suite 175
Phoenix AZ 85014
602-264-2157

Miller, Anderson & Sherrerd
Two Bala-Cynwyd Plaza
Bala Cynwyd PA 19004
215-668-0850

Mitchell Hutchins
(div. of Paine Webber)
140 Broadway
New York NY 10005
212-437-6755

Modern Portfolio Theory
   Associates Inc.
600 Fifth Ave. 8th floor
New York NY 10020
212-247-5858

Morgan Grenfell Investment
   Services Ltd.
520 Madison Ave. 39th floor
New York NY 10022
212-715-1700

Morgan Stanley Asset
  Mgmt., Inc.
(div. of Morgan Stanley)
1633 Broadway
New York NY 10019
212-974-2658

Mutual of America
666 Fifth Ave.
New York NY 10103
212-399-1600

Nat'l Investment Services of
  America, Inc.
P.O. Box 2143
Milwaukee WI 53201
414-271-6540

Neuberger & Berman
  Management, Inc.
522 Fifth Ave.
New York NY 10036
212-730-7370

Newton Funds
733 North Van Buren St.
Milwaukee WI 53202
414-271-0440

NSR Asset Management Corp.
605 Third Ave.
New York NY 10158
212-687-2200

Oppenheimer Capital Corp.
(investment counseling)
Oppenheimer Management
  Corp.
(mutual fund)
One New York Plaza
New York NY 10004
212-825-4000

Pacific Investment
  Management Co.
P.O. Box 9000
Newport Beach CA 92660
714-640-3031

Pioneering Management Corp.
60 State St.
Boston MA 02109
617-742-7825

T. Rowe Price Associates, Inc.
100 E. Pratt St.
Baltimore MD 21202
301-547-2000

The Putnam Management
  Co., Inc
(owned by Marsh & McLennan)
One Post Office Square
Boston MA 02109
617-292-1400

Redwood Capital Mgmt., Inc.
131 East Redwood St.
Baltimore MD 21202
301-727-8080

Rosenberg Capital Management
Four Embarcadero Center
Suite 2900
San Francisco CA 94111
415-954-5474

L.F. Rothschild Asset Mgmt.
(div. of L. F. Rothschild)
55 Water St.
New York NY 10041
212-412-1071

Roulston & Company, Inc.
4000 Chester Ave.
Cleveland OH 44103
216-431-3000

Frank Russell Investment
  Mgmt. Co.
P.O. Box 1591
Tacoma WA 98401-1591
206-627-7001

M.D. Sass Investors
  Services, Inc.
475 Park Ave. So.
New York NY 10016
212-532-6010

Schafer Capital Management Co.
645 5th Ave. 18th floor
New York NY 10022
212-644-1800

Schroder Capital Mgmt., Inc.
One State St.
New York NY 10004
212-269-6500

Scudder, Stevens & Clark
345 Park Ave.
New York NY 10154
212-350-8200
175 Federal St.
Boston MA 02110
617-482-3990
(also several other cities)

Sears Investment
  Management Co.
(div. of Sears)
55 West Monroe
Xerox Centre 32nd floor
Chicago IL 60603
312-875-0415

J. & W. Seligman & Co.
One Bankers Trust Plaza
New York NY 10006
212-775-1864

Shearson Lehman/American
  Express Asset Management
Two World Trade Center
Floor 106
New York NY 10048
212-321-6680

Shields Asset Management, Inc.
701 Westchester Ave.
Suite 201E
White Plains NY 10604
914-684-6900

Sirach/Flinn, Elvins Capital
  Mgmt.
3323 One Union Square
Seattle WA 98101
206-623-7955

Smith Barney, Harris Upham
  Capital Management
1345 Avenue of the Americas
New York NY 10105
212-399-6000

Smoot Knoche & Co.
Crandall Bldg. Suite 312
Salt Lake City UT 84101
801-328-4836

Standish, Ayer & Wood, Inc.
One Financial Center
Boston MA 02111
617-350-6100

State Street Research &
  Mgmt. Co.
(owed by Metropolitan Life)
One Financial Center
Boston MA 02111
617-482-3920

Stein Roe & Farnham
One South Wacker Drive
Chicago IL 60606
312-368-7700
(also several other cities)

Stralem & Company, Inc.
405 Park Ave.
New York NY 10022
212-888-8123

Strong/Corneliuson Capital
  Mgmt., Inc.
815 East Mason St. Suite 1610
Milwaukee WI 53202
414-765-0620

TCW Asset Management Co.
(sub. of Trust Co. of the West)
Mr. Glen Weirick
Director of Research
400 South Hope St.
Los Angeles CA 90071
213-683-4000

Templeton Investment
  Counsel, Ltd.
P.O. Box 3942
St. Petersburg FL 33731
813-823-8712

Thorndike, Doran,
  Paine & Lewis
28 State St.
Boston MA 02109
617-742-8100
233 Peachtree St. NE #700
Atlanta GA 30303
404-688-2782
(affiliate of Wellington
  Management Company)

Todd Investment Advisors
3160 First National Tower
Louisville KY 40202
502-585-3121

Torray Clark & Co. Inc.
6610 Rockledge Drive
Suite 450
Bethesda MD 20817
301-493-4600

Transamerica Investment
  Services Inc.
(sub. of Transamerica Corp.)
1150 South Olive St.
Los Angeles CA 90015
213-742-4141

Trident Investment Mgmt., Inc.
80 E. Ridgewood Ave.
Paramus NJ 07652
201-265-9600

Value Line Asset Management
711 Third Ave.
New York NY 10017
212-687-3965

The Vanguard Group, Inc.
P.O. Box 2600
Valley Forge PA 19482
215-648-6000

Vaughan, Nelson, Scarborough
  & McConnell, Inc.
6300 Texas Commerce Tower
Houston TX 77002
713-244-2545

Vilas Fischer Associates, Ltd.
One World Trade Center
Suite 1221
New York NY 10048
212-466-0710

Wall, Patterson, Hamilton &
  Allen, Inc.
900 Cain Tower
Atlanta GA 30043
404-659-6060

Warburg, Pincus
  Counsellors, Inc.
466 Lexington Ave.
New York NY 10017
212-878-0600

Weiss, Peck & Greer
One New York Plaza
New York NY 10004
212-908-9500

Wellington Management
  Company
(affiliate of Thorndike, Doran,
  Paine & Lewis)
28 State St.
Boston MA 02109
617-227-9500

Wentworth, Hauser & Violich,
  Inc.
333 Sacramento St.
San Francisco CA 94111
415-981-6911

Wertheim Asset Mgmt. Services
  Inc.
200 Park Ave.
New York NY 10166
212-578-0780

Wilkens & Nanovic Associates
102 Greenwich Ave.
Greenwich CT 06830
203-622-1040

Wilmington Capital Mgmt. Inc.
One Rodney Square Suite 807
Wilmington DE 19801
302-656-8241

Wright Investors' Service
10 Middle St.
Park City Plaza
Bridgeport CT 06604
203-333-6666

Insurance Companies

Where abbreviations for "Nat'l" and "Ins." have been used, be sure to write out the words "National" and "Insurance" when writing to these companies.

Aetna Life & Casualty Co.
Recruiting Office
151 Farmington Ave.
Hartford CT 06156
203-273-0123

Aid Association for Lutherans
Mr. Robert Hoffman
Employee Relations
4321 North Ballard Road
Appleton WI 54919
414-734-5721

Allstate Insurance Co.
Ms. Vilma Colon
Employment Center
Allstate Plaza
Northbrook IL 60062
312-291-7148

American General Life Ins. Co.
Nat'l. Life & Accident Ins. Co.
Mr. Thomas E. Hoppes
Personnel - 0363
Nashville TN 37250
615-749-1000

American National Ins. Co.
Ms. Janet Mitchell
Personnel Department
One Moody Plaza
Galveston TX 77550
409-763-4661

Bankers Life Company
Ms. Kris Jensen
Personnel Department
711 High St.
Des Moines IA 50307
515-247-5111

CNA Financial Corp.
Mr. Frank Jevitz
Employment Department
CNA Plaza
Chicago IL 60685
312-822-6934

Connecticut General Life Ins. Co.
Ms. Gerri M. Porter
Corporate University Relations
N87
Hartford CT 06152
203-726-5276

Connecticut Mutual Life Ins. Co.
Mr. Erik Kahn
Employment
140 Garden St.
Hartford CT 06154
203-727-6500

Equitable Life Assurance Society
    of the United States
Recruiting Department
40 Rector St.
New York NY 10006
212-513-4166

Executive Life Ins. Co.
Mr. Richard Palmer
Director of Personnel
P.O. Box 6090
Englewood CA 90312
213-312-1000

The Franklin Life Ins. Co.
Mrs. Toni Moore
Personnel Department
One Franklin Square
Springfield IL 62713
217-528-2011

General American Life Ins. Co.
Ms. Sally Lord
Personnel Department
P.O. Box 396
St. Louis MO 63101
314-231-1700

Guardian Life Ins. of America
Mrs. Ruth Klain
Human Resources 4B
201 Park Ave. So.
New York NY 10003
212-598-8400

John Hancock Mutual Life
  Ins. Co.
Mr. Randolph Smith
Personnel Department
P.O. Box 111
Boston MA 02117
617-421-6542

IDS Life Insurance Co.
Mr. Myrle Reiswig
Human Resources Dept.
700 IDS Tower
Minneapolis MN 55402
612-372-3131

Lincoln Nat'l Life Ins. Co.
Mr. Dennis Hollopeter
Corporate Recruiter
1300 So. Clinton
Fort Wayne IN 46801
219-427-3626

Lutheran Brotherhood
Mr. Karl Starr
Personnel Department
625 Fourth Ave So.
Minneapolis MN 55415
612-340-7054

Massachusetts Mutual Life
  Ins. Co.
Mrs. Shirley Carpenter
Personnel Department
1295 State St.
Springfield MA 01111
413-788-8411

Metropolitan Life Ins. Co.
Mr. Dan Beaton
Director of Recruiting
  and Staffing
One Madison Ave.
New York NY 10010
212-578-2113

Minnesota Mutual Life Ins. Co.
Mr. William Bush
Human Resources Dept.
400 North Robert St.
St. Paul MN 55101
612-298-3500

Mutual Benefit Life Ins. Co.
Ms. Nona Harris
Personnel Department
520 Broad St.
Newark NJ 07101
201-481-8000

Mutual of New York (MONY)
Mrs. Gretchen Green
Human Resources Dept.
1740 Broadway
New York NY 10019
212-708-2000

Mutual and United of Omaha Life
  Ins. Co.
Mr. Steven Howell
Personnel Department
Mutual of Omaha Plaza
Omaha NE 68175
402-342-7600

Nationwide Life Ins. Co.
Mr. Ray Mason
Employment Placement Office
One Nationwide Plaza
Columbus OH 43216
614-227-6419

New England Mutual Life
    Ins. Co.
Ms. Beverly Carris
Employment Consultant
501 Boylston St.
Boston MA 02117
617-266-3700

New York Life Insurance Co.
Mrs. Angela Coleman
Manager, Employment Division
51 Madison Ave.
New York NY 10010
212-576-7000

Northwestern Mutual Life
    Ins. Co.
Personnel Department
720 East Wisconsin Ave.
Milwaukee WI 53202
414-271-1444

Northwestern Nat'l Life Ins. Co.
Human Resource Dept.
Route 1511
20 Washington Ave. So.
Minneapolis MN 55440
612-372-1178

Ohio Nat'l Life Ins. Co.
Personnel Department
P.O. Box 237 #108
Cincinnati OH 45201
513-861-3600

Pacific Mutual Life Ins. Co.
Mr. Thomas Battaglia
700 Newport Center Drive
Newport Beach CA 92660
714-640-3527

Penn Mutual Life Ins. Co.
Mrs. Eileen Toogood
Human Resources Dept.
Independence Square
Philadelphia PA 19172
215-625-5000

Phoenix Mutual Life Ins. Co.
Mr. Trenton Mack
Personnel Department
One American Row
Hartford CT 06115
203-275-5512

Provident Mutual Life Ins. Co. of
    Philadelphia
Ms. Ann Price
Employment Administrator
1600 Market St.
Philadelphia PA 19101
215-636-5000

Prudential Insurance Company
    of America
Employment Office
213 Washington St.
Newark NJ 07101
201-877-6000

Security Benefit Life Ins. Co.
Ms. Julie McCullough
Human Resources Department
700 Harrison St.
Topeka KS 66636
913-295-3000

State Farm Life Ins. Co.
Ms. Nancy Mesropian
Personnel Employment
One State Farm Plaza
Bloomington IL 61701
309-766-6200

State Mutual of America
Mr. Carl A. Jacobson
Director of Employment &
  Employee Relations
440 Lincoln St.
Worcester MA 01605
617-852-1000

Sun Life Assurance Co. of
  Canada
Mr. Philip Manfra
Manager of Employment
One Sun Life Executive Park
Wellesley Hills MA 02181
617-237-6030

Teachers Insurance & Annuity
  Assoc.-College Retirement
  Equity Fund
Ms. Maureen McLaughlin
Personnel Department
730 Third Ave.
New York NY 10017
212-490-9000

Title Insurance & Trust Co.
Ms. Noreen Brown
Employment Department
6300 Wilshire Blvd.
Los Angeles CA 90048
213-852-6000

Transamerica Occidental Life
  Ins. Co.
Mr. Robert Conner
Employment & Placement
Box 2101 Terminal Annex
Los Angeles CA 90051
213-742-2111

The Travelers Insurance Co.
Personnel Division
Employment Section
One Tower Square
Hartford CT 06183
203-277-2994

The Union Central Life Ins. Co.
Personnel Office
P.O. Box 179
Cincinnati OH 45201
513-595-2508

Union Mutual Life Ins. Co.
Human Resources Office
P.O. Box 9548
Portland ME 04122
207-780-2211

Variable Annuity Life Ins. Co.
Mrs. Deborah House
American General Life Insurance
P.O. Box 1931
Houston TX 77001
713-522-1111

Western and Southern Life
  Ins. Co.
Mr. E. Channing Headley
Personnel Director
400 Broadway
Cincinnati OH 45202
513-629-1131

Financial Publications

Babson's Reports, Inc.
One Market St.
Wellesley Hills MA 02181
617-235-0900

Business Week
McGraw-Hill Inc.
Manager of Professional
  Recruitment
Human Resources Dept.
McGraw-Hill Bldg.
1221 Avenue of the Americas
New York NY 10020
212-512-2000

Capital Publishing Corporation
Two Laurel Avenue
P.O. Box 348
Wellesley Hills MA 02181
617-235-5405

Commerce Clearing House, Inc.
Mrs. Darde Gaertner
Personnel Director
4025 W. Peterson Ave.
Chicago IL 60646
312-583-8500

Dow Jones & Co. Inc.
(*The Wall Street Journal* and
  Barron's)
Ms. Charlene Watler
Personnel Department
420 Lexington Ave.
New York NY 10170
212-285-5000

Dun & Bradstreet Inc.
(Dun's Marketing)
Personnel Department
Three Century Drive
Parsippany NJ 07054
201-455-0900

Financial World
Mr. James Schiavone Sr. VP
1450 Broadway
New York NY 10018
212-869-1616

Forbes
Mr. James W. Michaels
Editor
60 Fifth Ave.
New York NY 10011
212-620-2200

Institutional Investor, Inc.
Ms. Nancy Cray
Personnel Department
488 Madison Ave.
New York NY 10022
212-303-3300

Investor's Daily
Mr. Steve Fox
Editorial Department
P.O. Box 25970
Los Angeles CA 90025
213-207-1832

Moody's Investor Service
Mr. Chip Conlin
Human Resources Department
99 Church St.
New York NY 10007
212-553-0300

Scripps-Howard Business
  Journals
Mr. Jack Nettis
Director of Employee Relations
5314 Bingle Road
Houston TX 77092
713-688-8811

Standard & Poor's
   Corporation
Mr. Gregory Myers
Human Resources Department
25 Broadway
New York NY 10004
212-208-8669

United Business Service
   Company
210 Newbury St.
Boston MA 02116
617-267-8855

The Value Line Investment Survey
Value Line, Inc.
Personnel Department
711 Third Ave.
New York NY 10017
212-687-3965

Wiesenberger Financial Services
(Warren, Gorham & Lamont)
Ms. Judy Damore
Human Resources Dept.
1633 Broadway
New York NY 10019
212-977-7444

Miscellaneous Financial Services
Including Real Estate

The Associates
(business financing)
Mr. Ralph Hood
Director of Human Resources
The Associates Center
150 North Michigan Ave.
Chicago IL 60601
312-781-5800

Coldwell Banker-Capital
  Management Services
(real estate)
Mr. Thomas Townley
Personnel Department
533 Fremont Ave.
Los Angeles CA 90071
213-613-3491

CompuServe
(financial information)
Ms. Tammy Johnson
Human Resources Dept.
5000 Arlington Centre Blvd.
Columbus OH 43220
614-457-8600

Corporate Property Investors
(real estate)
Mr. Hans Mautner
President
305 E. 47th St.
New York NY 10017
212-421-8200

EASTDIL
(real estate)
Mr. Terry Sternberg
650 California St.
San Francisco CA 94108
415-788-3232
40 West 57th St.
New York NY 10019
212-397-2700

Federal National Mortgage
  Association (Fannie Mae)
Human Resources Dept.
3900 Wisconsin Ave. N.W.
Washington, D.C. 20016
202-537-7000

First Winthrop Corp.
(real estate)
Ms. Nancy Spokowski
Personnel Department
225 Franklin St.
Boston MA 02110
617-482-6200

JMB Realty Corp.
(real estate)
Ms. Roseann Miksanek
Personnel Dept. Suite 1400
875 North Michigan Ave.
Chicago IL 60611
312-440-6972

D. F. King & Co., Inc.
(information agent)
Mr. Cole Brundage
Treasurer
60 Broad Street
New York NY 10004
212-269-5550

The McGrath Company
(real estate)
Ms. Regina McGrath
2500 Michelson Drive
Suite 250
Irvine CA 92715
714-476-0771

Monex International, Ltd.
(precious metals)
Mr. Abraham Cancel
Payroll Administrator
4910 Birch St.
Newport Beach CA 92660
714-752-1400

Victor Palmieri and Co., Inc.
(real estate)
Mr. John A. Koskinen
2021 K St. N.W. Suite 700
Washington DC 20006
202-223-8690

Pandick, Inc.
(financial printing)
Ms. Eileen Stewart
Personnel Manager
345 Hudson St.
New York NY 10014
212-741-5555
Pandick New England
647 Summer St.
Boston MA 02210
617-269-7222
(many other offices)

Venture Capital

In contacting venture capital companies, it is best to contact one of the partners directly. Obtain their names from a venture capital directory (see "Resources") or by calling the firms directly.

Adler & Company
375 Park Ave.
New York NY 10152
212-759-2800

R. W. Allsop & Associates
2750 First Ave. N.E.
Cedar Rapids IA 52402
319-363-8971

American Research
  & Development
(div. of Textron)
45 Milk St.
Boston MA 02109
617-423-7500

Ampersand Management
  Company
(div. of Paine Webber)
100 Federal St. 31st floor
Boston MA 02110
617-423-8000

Arscott, Norton & Associates
375 Forest Ave.
Palo Alto CA 94301
415-853-0766

Bessemer Venture Partners
630 Fifth Ave.
New York NY 10111
212-708-9300

Bradford Associates
22 Chambers St.
Princeton NJ 08540
609-921-3880

Brentwood Associates
11661 San Vicente Boulevard
Los Angeles CA 90049
213-826-6581

Burr, Egan, Deleage & Co., Inc.
One Post Office Square
Boston MA 02110
617-482-8020
3 Embarcadero Center Suite 2560
San Francisco CA 94111
415-362-4022

Cable, Howse & Cozadd
999 3rd Ave. Suite 4300
Seattle WA 98104
206-583-2700

Capital Southwest Corp.
12900 Preston Road #700
Dallas TX 75230
214-233-8242

Chappell & Co.
One Lombard St.
San Francisco CA 94111
415-397-5094

The Charles River Partnership
133 Federal St. Suite 602
Boston MA 02110
617-482-9370

Citicorp Venture Capital, Ltd.
(sub. of Citicorp)
One Sansone St.
San Francisco CA 94104
415-627-6000
153 E. 53rd St. 28th floor
New York NY 10043
212-559-1127

Concord Partners
(sub. of Dillon Read)
535 Madison Ave.
New York NY 10022
212-906-7000

DSV Partners III
221 Nassau St.
Princeton NJ 08542
609-924-6420

First Capital Corp. of Chicago
(sub. of First Chicago Corp.)
3 First Nat'l Plaza Suite 1330
Chicago IL 60670
312-732-5400

First Venture Capital Corp.
  of Boston
(sub. of Bank of Boston)
100 Federal St.
Boston MA 02110
617-434-4481

Frontenac Venture Company
208 South LaSalle
Chicago IL 60604
312-368-0044

General Electric Venture
  Capital Corporation
(sub. of General Electric)
3135 Easton Turnpike
Fairfield CT 06431
203-373-2211

Golder, Thoma & Cressey
120 S. LaSalle St.
Chicago IL 60603
312-853-3322

Greyhound Capital Corp.
(sub. of The Greyhound Corp.)
Greyhound Tower
Phoenix AZ 85077
602-222-8200

Greylock Management Corp.
One Federal St.
Boston MA 02110
617-423-5525

Hambrecht & Quist, Inc.
235 Montgomery St.
San Francisco CA 94104
415-986-5500

Harrison Capital, Inc.
(sub. of Texaco, Inc.)
2000 Westchester Ave.
Harrison NY 10650
914-253-7845

Harvest Ventures, Inc.
767 3rd Ave. 7th floor
New York NY 10017
212-838-7776

Heizer Corporation
20 North Wacker Drive
Chicago IL 60606
312-641-2200

Hellman, Ferri Investment
  Associates
One Post Office Square
Boston MA 02109
617-482-7735

Hixon Venture Company
300 Convent St.
Suite 1400
San Antonio TX 78205
512-225-3053

Idanta Partners
3344 North Torrey Pines Court
La Jolla CA 92037
817-338-2020

Inco Securities Corp.
(sub. of Inco Ltd.)
One New York Plaza
New York NY 10004
212-742-4000

Innoven Capital
Park 80 Plaza West 1
Saddlebrook NJ 07662
201-845-4900

Institutional Venture Partners
3000 Sand Hill Road
Bldg. 2 #290
Menlo Park CA 94025
415-854-0132

InterFirst Venture Corp.
(sub. of InterFirst Bank)
P.O. Box 83000
Dallas TX 75283-0644
214-977-3166

InterWest Partners
2620 Augustine Drive #201
Santa Clara CA 95054
408-727-7200

Kleiner, Perkins, Caufield
  & Byers
Four Embarcadero Center
Suite 3520
San Francisco CA 94111
415-421-3110

Carl Marks & Company, Inc.
77 Water St.
New York NY 10005
212-437-7080

Massachusetts Capital
  Resource Co.
545 Boylston St. #1100
Boston MA 02116
617-536-3900

Mayfield Fund
2200 Sand Hill Road
Menlo Park CA 94025
415-854-5560

Memorial Drive Trust
(affil. Arthur D. Little, Inc.)
20 Acorn Park
Cambridge MA 02140
617-864-5770

Menlo Ventures
3000 Sand Hill Road
Bldg. 4 #100
Menlo Park CA 94025
415-854-8540

Merrill, Pickard, Anderson
  and Eyre
(sub. of Bank of America Corp.)
Two Palo Alto Square Suite 425
Palo Alto CA 94306
415-856-8880

Morgan, Holland
  Management Corp.
One Liberty Square
Boston MA 02109
617-423-1765

Narragansett Capital Corp.
40 Westminster St.
Providence RI 02903
401-751-1000

New Court Securities Corp.
(sub. of Rothschild, Inc.)
One Rockefeller Plaza
New York NY 10020
212-757-6000

New Enterprise Associates
1119 St. Paul St.
Baltimore MD 21202
301-244-0115

Norwest Venture Capital Mgmt.
(sub. Northwest Bancorporation)
2800 Piper Jaffray Tower
222 So. 9th St.
Minneapolis MN 55402-3388
612-372-8770

About the Author

Mary E. Calhoun retired from her career as a stockbroker to write this book. A graduate of Wellesley College, she spent nine years as an Account Executive in Boston with Merrill Lynch and Hambrecht & Quist. While at Merrill Lynch, she rose to become one of the most successful brokers in New England, specializing in corporate financial services, including acting as liaison with investment banking.

She has worked extensively with college students, helping them prepare for financial careers by providing counseling and seminars, as well as programs with other financial professionals.